ISSUES THAT CONCERN YOU

Teen Homelessness

H. Craig Erskine III, *Book Editor*

GREENHAVEN
PUBLISHING

362.775
TEE

Published in 2018 by Greenhaven Publishing, LLC
353 3rd Avenue, Suite 255, New York, NY 10010

Copyright © 2018 by Greenhaven Publishing, LLC

First Edition

Articles in Greenhaven Publishing anthologies are often edited for length to meet page requirements. In addition, original titles of these works are changed to clearly present the main thesis and to explicitly indicate the author's opinion. Every effort is made to ensure that Greenhaven Publishing accurately reflects the original intent of the authors. Every effort has been made to trace the owners of the copyrighted material.

Cataloging-in-Publication Data

Names: Erskine, H. Craig, III, editor.
Title: Teen homelessness / edited by H. Craig Erskine III.
Description: New York : Greenhaven Publishing, 2018. I Series: Issues that concern you I Includes bibliographical references and index. I Audience: Grades 9 to 12.
Identifiers: LCCN ISBN 9781534502260 (library bound) IISBN 9781534502796 (pbk.)
Subjects: LCSH: Homeless teenagers--Juvenile literature. I Homelessness--Juvenile literature.
Classification: LCC HV4493.H65528 2018 I DDC 362.7/75692083--dc23

Manufactured in the United States of America

Website: http://greenhavenpublishing.com

CONTENTS

The National Runaway Switchboard estimates that on any given night there are approximately 1.3 million homeless youth living unsupervised on the streets, in abandoned buildings, with friends, or with strangers. Homeless youth are at a higher risk for physical abuse, sexual exploitation, mental health disabilities, substance abuse, and death. It is estimated that 5,000 unaccompanied youth will die each year as a result of assault, illness, or suicide.

Homeless youth are typically defined as unaccompanied young people aged 12 and over who do not have a permanent place to stay and who are living in shelters, on the street, in cars or vans, or vacant buildings, or are "couch surfing," or otherwise living in unstable circumstances. The Runaway and Homeless Youth Act (RHYA), administered by the Family and Youth Services Bureau and funded by the Department of Health and Human Services' Administration for Children and Families, defines homeless youth as individuals who are "not more than 21 years of age…for whom it is not possible to live in a safe environment with a relative and who have no other safe alternative living arrangement."

The US Department of Education defines homeless youth as youth who "lack a fixed, regular, and nighttime residence," or an "individual who has a primary nighttime residence that is: a) a supervised or publically operated shelter designed to provide temporary living accommodation; b) an institution that provides a temporary residence for individuals intended to be institutionalized including welfare hotels, congregate shelters and transitional housing for the mentally ill; or c) a public or private place not designed for, or ordinarily used as a regular sleeping accommodation for human beings."

Teen homelessness has many faces, from the young member of a family that has been evicted from their home due to substance abuse, or gambling addictions by one or both of the parents, or just from existing in the depths of poverty. The family may be living out of a car or van and roaming between parks and interstate rest areas. To the young teen who has run away – escaping physical, emotional, or even sexual abuse, or other family violence. To the teenager who has finally revealed his or her sexual orientation to their religious, ultra-conservative parents, only to be banished from their presence. To the young girl who leaves home rather than face her parents, or becomes pregnant while she is out on the street. Teen homelessness wears the face of all ages, all orientations, and all ethnicities.

A report, by the Office of Juvenile Justice and Delinquency Prevention, in the US Department of Justice, published in 2002, estimated 1.7 million homeless and runaway youth were equally divided among males and females, with the majority of them between the ages of 15 and 17. According to the US Conference of Mayors, in 2005, unaccompanied youth accounted for 3% of the urban homeless population. The National Network of Runaway and Youth Services states 6 percent of homeless youth are LGBTQ. Ten percent of homeless youth were recorded as pregnant (Greene and Ringwalt, 1998). All of these individuals, collectively, become potential victims of further exploitation, or even human trafficking.

Human trafficking is commonly referred to as a form of modern-day slavery in which people profit from controlling and exploiting others. According to the US Department of Homeland Security, traffickers use "force, fraud or coercion" to lure their victims and force them into labor or prostitution. The victims then get arrested for a variety of crimes, including soliciting, chronic truancy, possession of drugs, public indecency, and assault. They also face contact with alcohol and many types of drugs, and they risk exposure to STDs and other viral infections with few options for treatment. Some even lose their life.

Homelessness among young people continues to remain a serious social issue today. The consequences of ignorance and silence cannot be ignored. Youth homelessness and its consequences are not just problems for those involved, but for society in general and the cost to society is high. States spend approximately $5.7 billion each year to incarcerate youth for a non-violent offence such as homelessness. Furthermore, the problems and barriers these youth face clearly hinder their ability to become contributing, successful members of their families and society. If they don't receive the help they need while they're young, they may very well become tomorrow's chronically homeless adults.

The issues related to teen homelessness are not without their controversies. For example, the foster care system is meant to take in orphaned and disadvantaged youths and provide for their wellbeing. But in some cases the very organizations set up to help them abuse them and they run away to escape. The situation may lead the vulnerable teen to become a gang member for a sense of belonging.

What is society's responsibility? There are many conflicting views on this topic. Some believe that social welfare encourages dependency. Others believe that social welfare programs help those truly in need. Some believe that communities should build more homeless shelters, while others believe that such shelters encourage complacency, increase crime, and lower surrounding home values.

Teen homelessness does not only affect the young people who find themselves without a stable living situation. Because homeless teens are associated with criminal futures and possible incarceration, lower education levels, psychological and physical health issues, and bleak employment prospects, teen homelessness is a societal problem. If there is debate over whether or not a society is responsible for ensuring the safety and stability of its children, there is no question that society will end up paying the price sooner or later.

The viewpoints in *Issues That Concern You: Teen Homelessness* explore complicated but important issues at the heart of teen homelessness. Students will be exposed to a variety of perspectives that explore the causes, effects, and potential solutions of this problem.

ONE

Homelessness Among the Families of Our Veterans Must Be Addressed

Roya Ijadi-Maghsoodi

An effort to reduce homelessness among US veterans has met with some success, but researchers are concerned that veterans' families are slipping through the cracks. In the following viewpoint, Roya Ijadi-Maghsoodi argues that homeless veterans with families are often overlooked because they are missed in homeless counts. Not only have the heads of these families sacrificed a great deal to serve their country, but their children face unique challenges including homelessness. These families deserve medical, educational, and social support for their own sake, as well as society's. Ijadi-Maghsoodi is Assistant Professor of Psychiatry and Biobehavioral Sciences/Investigator at the VA Greater Los Angeles HSR&D Center for the Study of Healthcare Innovation, Implementation & Policy, University of California, Los Angeles.

In 2010, the Obama administration announced the ambitious goal of ending homelessness among veterans. Over the last year, the number of veterans who are homeless dropped 30 percent in Los Angeles County. Nationwide, veteran homelessness fell by almost 50 percent since 2009.

A high percentage of US veterans are homeless and have children in their custody. Children in these families suffer in many ways.

Yet statistics are only part of the story. What is missing from federal and state statistics, the media and the minds of many Americans, is the story of homeless veteran families.

Through my work as a researcher and physician caring for women and homeless veterans, I see these families. I hear about their struggles to find housing in safe neighborhoods instead of Skid Row, where their children are exposed to violence and drug use.

Overlooking Veterans with Families

Families are often missed when volunteers head out to count homeless individuals. Veterans with families often stay with friends, known as "doubling up." Or, forced to fragment, parents send kids to stay with family while they go to a shelter.

Plus, some females who are homeless and the head of their household don't identify as veterans. They may not be eligible for Veterans Affairs (VA) benefits, or are unclear about available services. Some may not seek care at the VA due to mistrust, harassment or past military sexual trauma.

Providers, policymakers and the public need to understand that homelessness among the families of men and women who have served our nation may be invisible. But it is significant.

Limited studies point to higher rates of veteran family homelessness than expected from the counts. Nineteen percent of families served by Supportive Services for Veteran Families in the FY 2015 had at least one child. A study of veterans receiving VA homeless services by Tsai and colleagues showed that nine percent of literally homeless male veterans – those living on the streets or uninhabitable locations – and 18 percent of unstably housed male veterans had children in their custody. A striking 30 percent of literally homeless female veterans, as well as 45 percent of unstably housed female veterans, had children in their custody.

Causes of Homelessness

What contributes to homelessness among veteran families?

First, homelessness among women veterans is rising. Eleven percent of military personnel who served in Operation Iraqi Freedom/Operation Enduring Freedom (OIF/OEF) were women, the largest number involved in combat operations in U.S. history.

Women veterans are more likely to be mothers and mothers at a younger age than civilians, and more likely to receive lower income than male veterans.

They face high rates of trauma, especially military sexual trauma, a known risk for homelessness.

And, strikingly, women veterans are up to four times more likely to be homeless than civilian women.

Male veterans returning from OIF/OEF tend to be younger and may have young families. As of 2010, 49 percent of deployed

Homelesss Veterans with Families

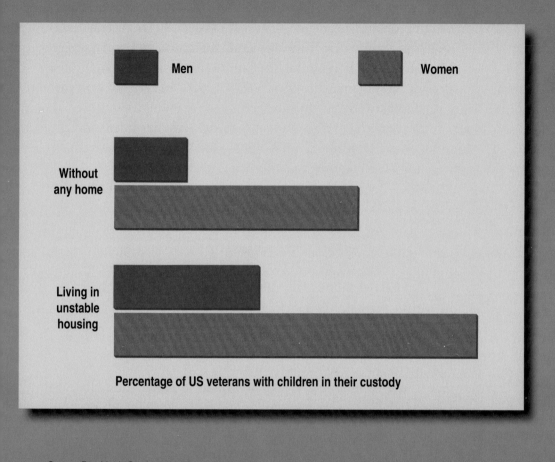

Men

Women

Without any home

Living in unstable housing

Percentage of US veterans with children in their custody

Source: Psychiatric Services (2015)

service members had children. They also have a higher prevalence of PTSD, compared to veterans of other wars. This is thought to be associated with an increased risk for homelessness.

To make matters worse, our country is in the grips of an affordable housing crisis. In California, we have only 21 homes available for every 100 extremely low-income households. And every day, families face discrimination searching for housing due to their race or ethnicity, being a veteran or using a voucher.

What Homeless Veteran Families Need

These families are at high risk. Decades of research show that children in homeless families are at risk for physical and mental health problems, academic delay and of becoming homeless themselves as adults – creating a second generation of homelessness. Many homeless veteran families are resilient, but face additional stressors of reintegrating into civilian society and coping with parents who may have PTSD and traumatic brain injuries.

Our team has been conducting interviews to understand the needs of veteran families who are homeless. We also formed a work group of recently homeless veteran parents.

We are finding that, although veterans are often satisfied with their own health and mental health services at the VA, many parents feel alone when it comes to their family.

Many veterans are overwhelmed by PTSD and depression, as well as the search to find housing and a job. They worry about the toll on their family. Yet they find few resources for their family within the VA, such as family therapy, and need help finding needed health and mental health care for their spouse and children in the community.

Parents need more help connecting to resources for their families in the community, clearer information about the social services available to veteran families and more emotional support as parents.

Moving Forward

We need to change the conversation when we talk about homeless veterans. We need to talk about homeless veteran families.

These families are in our communities, the children are attending public schools, their parents are trying to work multiple jobs or attend college and many receive care in our VA and community clinics.

Within the VA, we need to consider the whole family and provide more connection to the community to help families succeed. At the VA Greater Los Angeles Healthcare System West Los Angeles Medical Center, a new family wellness center will open as a collaborative effort between UCLA and the VA. The center will serve as a hub to strengthen veteran families, through services such as family and couple resilience programs, parenting skills workshops and connection to community services. More efforts are needed to engage families who may need it most.

Beyond the VA, we need enhanced understanding and empathy for veteran families with homelessness within the community. This involves greater understanding of the needs of these children in schools. We should also find ways to help veteran families dealing with PTSD integrate into the community after being homeless.

And most of all, we need to increase access to affordable housing in safe neighborhoods for these families.

The recent wars may seem over for many Americans, but they are far from over for our homeless veteran families. We owe it to them to do better.

TWO

Government Policy Makes Homelessness Worse

Tracy C. Miller

> Who is more effective in addressing problems like teen homelessness: the government or private organizations? In the following viewpoint Tracy Miller states that homelessness is influenced by incentives and that government-subsidized housing for the poor may make the problem worse. He notes that a lack of affordable housing may contribute to homelessness but problems with alcohol, drug abuse, or mental illness are also contributing factors. Government programs that provide skills and treatment to overcome addictions and psychoses are expensive and have low rates of success while private programs have a higher success rate. Miller is a fellow for economic theory and policy with the Center for Vision and Values. He holds a Ph.D. from University of Chicago.

During a recent trip to Chicago, I couldn't help but notice the large number of homeless people in the downtown area, including one homeless man pushing a child in a stroller. Homelessness was frequently discussed during the 1980s, but seems to receive less media attention now. And yet, the number of homeless today is approximately twice as large as it was in the 1980s.

Homelessness, like any other social problem, is influenced by incentives. Unfortunately, government policy may actually be

"Homelessness: How Government Policy Makes It Worse," by Tracy Miller, The Center for Vision & Values at Grove City College, May 25, 2012. Reprinted by permission.

Many believe that help from private, community, and faith-based organizations is the best solution to the homelessness problem.

making the problem worse, particularly government-subsidized housing for the poor.

Government Shelters

Many cities have constructed homeless shelters to provide a place for the homeless to stay out of the cold. By the late 1980s, governments created a network of shelters and soup kitchens to feed and house between 200,000 and 300,000 people per day. Between 1988 and 1996, some 275,000 permanent and transitional housing units intended for homeless persons were added. By 1996, roughly 607,000 beds were available as part of the homeless service system in the United States.

There is little evidence to suggest that government-provided shelter has in any way solved or even reduced the problem of homelessness—to the contrary, as noted, the total number of homeless

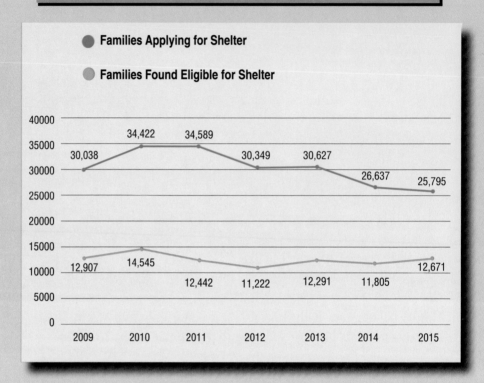

Shelter Applications and Eligibility for Families with Children

● Families Applying for Shelter

● Families Found Eligible for Shelter

Source: Department of Homeless Services

has risen. While advocates for the homeless recognize this, many believe that providing other forms of government assistance will help people avoid homelessness or escape it. In their view, helping people get government-funded rental assistance, food stamps, and welfare checks is integral to preventing homelessness. Some contend that supplying the homeless and those at risk of becoming homeless with permanent housing at government expense will get homeless people off the streets so they can live stable lives.

In truth, lack of affordable housing is not the main reason that people become homeless, although it may be a contributing factor in some cities. People sometimes become homeless due to habits or addictions that lead to mismanagement of their finances, unstable family relationships, and the inability to keep a regular job. According to Martha Burt of the Urban Institute, three quarters of those who are homeless report having problems with alcohol, drug abuse, or mental illness.

Encouraging Homelessness

Oftentimes, providing government-funded services to the homeless with no strings attached only makes it easier for some of them to continue their bad habits, whether the problem is substance abuse or an unwillingness to accept responsibility for personal behavior. This explains why homelessness did not decline but increased between the early 1980s and 2007, even though the economy was booming and unemployment and poverty were declining. Christopher Jencks argues that shelters made homelessness less painful; this meant that the homeless were "less willing to sacrifice their pride, their self-respect or their cocaine fix to avoid" homelessness. For many people, the availability of shelters seems to increase the incentive to become homeless rather than (if possible) choosing to live with a relative or friend.

Not only does the availability of temporary shelters frequently encourage homelessness, but so does federal housing policy. Many single-parent families would like to move into government-subsidized housing. Because it is in short supply, they would have to wait years for a subsidized apartment to open up. By becoming homeless, a family who was living in someone else's home can move to the front of the line for government-subsidized housing.

Likewise, another form of government assistance is problematic: Government programs that try to provide people with skills and treatment to overcome addictions and psychoses are expensive and have low rates of success. The success rate of some private programs to help the homeless is much higher than government programs—as high as 85 percent. While government programs continue to be funded even if they are ineffective, private charitable organizations' long-term survival depends on getting good results. Successful private programs usually continue to attract donors and volunteers, including former homeless people who themselves have been helped.

It is only natural to feel sympathy for the plight of the homeless. The solution to homelessness, however, is not more handouts from government. Homelessness can be prevented or overcome when a caring community helps those at risk to develop self-discipline and a good work ethic. This is not easy to do, but some private organizations are already doing good work in this area. Those organizations might grow and multiply and also be more effective if government programs, which often interfere with private efforts, were scaled back or eliminated.

THREE

Policy Should Be Based on Reality, Not Rhetoric

Acton Institute

> Teens of homeless families are often victims of a broken welfare system. In the following viewpoint, the Acton Institute shares the writing of two individuals serving in the Department of Health and Human Services who argue that the multiplicity of government programs offer an open invitation to fraud, and that federal benefits discourage work, encourage dependency, and undercut families. The two writers state that welfare enables teens to leave school, have children, and eschew work. They point out that genuine reform requires asking not just at what level—federal or state—welfare policy should be determined, but whether government should be making policy at all, or whether charity should be left to private individuals, families, communities, and institutions. The Acton Institute is a think-tank that promotes individual liberty and a free society.

American political discourse has coarsened in recent years. Perhaps nowhere is this more evident than with the issue of poverty. As Mary Jo Bane and David T. Ellwood, both currently serving in the Department of Health and Human Services, put it, "when the topic of welfare comes up, dialogue often turns angry and judgmental; the prose becomes purple."

Yet purple prose almost seems appropriate when dealing with today's welfare system. It is, as many contend, overly expensive;

The debate about whether welfare helps families get on their feet or encourages dependence has been going on for decades.

the multiplicity of programs offer an open invitation to fraud. The federal benefits discourage work, encourage dependency, and undercut families. Others charge that the current system is patronizing and even dehumanizing. Americans are rightly disappointed with government's care of the poor.

Into this swamp step Bane and Ellwood. Though hailing from the liberal side of the political spectrum, they've produced a book which largely steers clear of ideological shoals. Rather, they focus on presenting the reality behind the rhetoric, on which policy should be based.

Welfare Does Not Promote Independence

They begin by describing the nature of the welfare system itself. In the early 1960's it relied on what they call the "casework model", focusing on home visits. Then came several years of "the legal rights movement", based on the rather curious assumption that grantees had a higher moral claim to benefits than did taxpayers to their earnings. Then, write Bane and Ellwood, came "bureaucratization" through 1988, when Congress passed the Family Support Act, in an attempt to promote independence and self-sufficiency. Alas, the latter had only limited impact. Conclude the authors: welfare programs aimed at getting the recipient back into the work place, in certain circumstances, can have dramatic results. But dramatic change is the exception, not the rule.

Bureaucracies and regulations are not neutral, but create incentives. What, then, has been the impact of welfare on program beneficiaries? The answer should determine the direction of reform. As Bane and Ellwood explain: "If welfare is predominantly a short-term aid, with people moving quickly into private sources of support, then welfare is best understood as a transitional program. Dependency becomes less a worry, and policies designed to move people from welfare to work might be unnecessary ... But if welfare lasts a very long time, then the nature and the reasons for long-term use become important, and policy responses more complex."

Unfortunately, the dynamics of welfare are extraordinarily complex. Just 14 percent of spells on welfare last ten or more years. Yet 48 percent of current recipients move into and out of the program fairly quickly, a large number of chronic recipients dominate the system. The average number of years a woman will receive AFDC is twelve; more than half the current recipients at any one time will average ten years or more on welfare. The problem is particularly acute for single parents: "most unmarried mothers will eventually have relatively long durations." Thus, while Bane and Ellwood argue that both liberals and conservatives are wrong about welfare dependency, the facts seem to point more to the right: although welfare does not ensnare the majority

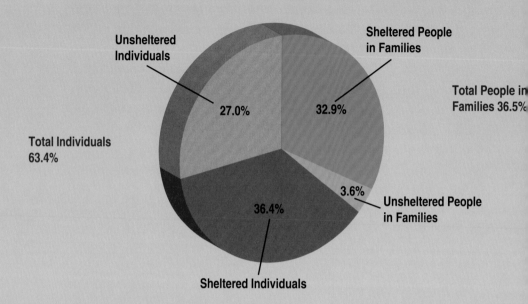

Homeless population by household type and sheltered status, 2015

Unsheltered Individuals 27.0%

Sheltered People in Families 32.9%

Total People in Families 36.5%

Total Individuals 63.4%

3.6%
Unsheltered People in Families

36.4%
Sheltered Individuals

Source: HUD, via Boston University

of its users, it does encourage dependency by many of the most vulnerable recipients. As Bane and Ellwood acknowledge, "race, education, marital status, work experience, and disability status all have especially strong relationships with welfare dynamics."

Unfortunately, the middle three are all affected by the existence of welfare, since it enables teenagers to leave school, have children, eschew work, all the while forming separate households. Fully one-third of welfare recipients who were unmarried when they started on AFDC will collect benefits for at least ten years. Similar percentages of those who were under the age of 22, dropped out of high school, and had no recent work experience will also be on welfare for ten or more years. When these characteristics coincide — a recipient is both unmarried and a high school drop out — the likelihood of dependence rises sharply.

Thus, the authors advocate two basic steps, both "identifying long-term recipients and considering the cost-effectiveness of the proposed intervention." They emphasize the importance of targeting, since "one size cannot possibly fit all welfare recipients." They warn policymakers not to wait to see which recipients become long-term recipients. In practice this means directing employment, training, and other programs at young women with young children when they first apply for welfare. Bane and Ellwood also urge working "as hard at keeping people off as one does at getting them off."

Sensible policies all, yet Bane's and Ellwood's research suggests that welfare caseloads are largely impervious to this sort of tinkering. Today, three of ten recipients escape welfare by marriage. Another ten percent exit when their children move beyond eligibility age. Twelve percent leave the rolls because other transfer income, such as disability payments, rise. In contrast, just one-quarter of "exits", by one reckoning, reflect increased earnings, though Bane and Ellwood cite additional studies that indicate this figure may understate the actual number. So long as welfare's basic incentive structure remains intact, policymakers are not likely to have a dramatic impact on the basic decisions that give rise to poverty — leaving school, failing to marry, having children out of wedlock, and so on.

How to Achieve Self-Sufficiency

Bane and Ellwood similarly dissect the problem of dependency. They review several competing models: rational choice (recipients weigh costs and benefits); expectancy (people's belief in their control over their destiny); and culture (personal, family, and community values). They conclude that "of the three models, the choice framework seems most effective in explaining the results, but that there are enough anomalies in the data to warrant looking beyond the pure choice model." This finding merely reinforces the argument that Congress needs to change the system's underlying incentives, which currently reward failure to form families, work, and finish school, all the while bearing children. The authors warn that past initiatives to promote work have had only a limited nature of reforms: "the results clearly suggest that modest changes in benefit policy (either liberalizing or tightening) in the range countenanced in relevant political debate, are unlikely to have major impacts on work and dependency. Other policy directions may be more fruitful."

The authors go on to advance their proposals to increase self-sufficiency. Particularly important, in their view, is ensuring that people who work are not poor. As they report: "After government transfers, poor two-parent families with a full-time worker have incomes farther below the poverty line than single parent families on welfare or two parent families with an unemployed worker. The working poor are literally the poorest of the poor." As a result, they endorse the Earned Income Tax Credit and more effective child support enforcement.

Sensible as such steps might seem — and there is no serious argument against making fathers pay to support their children — they do not address the core problem of the welfare system: perverse incentives. Genuine reform requires more than tinkering; it requires reconsidering who should be eligible for what benefits when. Genuine reform also requires asking not just at what level, federal or state, welfare policy should be determined, but whether government should be making policy at all — whether charity should be left to private individuals, families, communities, and institutions.

Bane and Ellwood do not ask, let alone attempt to answer, these questions, so their solutions fall painfully short. Yet their thorough research and analysis will help policymakers who do ask such questions design new policies that might make a difference. In this way *Welfare Realities* should help Americans see through the purple prose that so often characterizes the welfare debate.

FOUR

Teen Homelessness Is Disproportionately High for Minorities

L. Michael Gipson

> Teens who are part of oppressed communities have unique obstacles to overcome in order to fulfill their potential. In the following excerpted viewpoint L. Michael Gipson focuses on the challenges faced by LGBTQ teens of color, who often are at risk for poverty, homelessness, disease, incarceration, and violence. The author contends that this community may be the most vulnerable of any other youth population in terms of negative health and developmental outcome because of the likelihood they will experience prejudice and discrimination on multiple fronts on the basis of their individual and collective identities. Gipson was until recently the racial and economic justice coordinator of the National Youth Advocacy Coalition.

In a capitalist society that places a premium on young adulthood (read: economic productivity and opportunity), reproductive capacity and propensity, masculinity, European lineage, conformity to strict gender roles ageism, sexism, racial prejudice and discrimination, transphobia, homophobia, and heterosexism will flourish. In a society that has disdain for racial and ethnic complexity, gender variance and sexual diversity, intolerance is the likely experience and oppression the probable condition for

"Poverty, Race and LGBT Youth," by L. Michael Gipson, Poverty & Race Research Action Council, March/April, 2002. Reprinted by permission.

Teens in minority groups are more likely to find themselves homeless because they have more obstacles to overcome.

people who belong to communities that defy simplistic categorization, resist the values and ideals of the majority community, and consistently engage in political protest against the political and cultural dominance of those belonging to the status quo. For people from these communities, outcomes often include an increased potential to experience poverty, disease, incarceration and violence. In the US, these communities are easily identified as the poor, youth, the elderly, racial and ethnic minorities, women and those identifying as lesbian, gay, bisexual and transgendered (LGBT). Members of an oppressed community have unique obstacles to overcome in order to fulfill their potential. For individuals like LGBT youth of color (YOC) whose identities cross the lines of age, racial or ethnic identity, sexual orientation, gender and/or non-conformist gender expression, and low socio-economic status, the challenge of achieving resiliency, economic prosperity, a healthy existence, and the privileges of full citizenship are markedly reduced. Consequently, LGBT YOC may be the most vulnerable of any other youth population in terms of negative health and developmental outcomes because of a lack of research determining the needs and addressing the health status of the population; a lack of support either from their cultural communities and their LGBT community; an over-representation in the child welfare and juvenile justice system; and the likelihood they will experience prejudice and discrimination on multiple fronts on the basis of their individual and collective identities.

Who are LGBT YOC?

While research on LGBT youth in general is scarce, research on LGBT YOC is virtually nonexistent. In a 2001 review of the professional literature and research needs of LGBT YOC commissioned by the National Youth Advocacy Coalition, researcher Caitlin Ryan discovered only 16 studies (14 articles and 2 book chapters) published during the last 30 years on LGBT YOC. Most of these were empirical studies, with small sample sizes, samples of convenience or snowball samples that lack diversity in terms of class, geographic area and level of acculturation.

LGBT YOC data are also unlikely to be extracted from national data sources. National or government-sponsored studies on youth behaviors like the Department of Health and Human Services Youth Risk Behavior Survey (YRBS) that routinely ask questions about heterosexual sexual risk-taking behaviors do not ask youth questions about same sex behavior or desires for fear that states already hostile to the data collection process and the politically charged outcomes of the survey's behavioral findings will not implement the survey tools and collect the necessary data. Some states, like Massachusetts, and municipalities, like New York City, do ask a few questions about same sex behavior among youth on

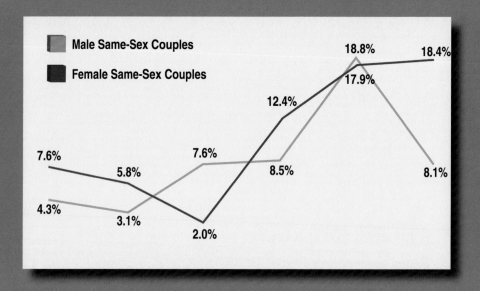

Percent of LGBTQ People of Color Living in Poverty

Male Same-Sex Couples

Female Same-Sex Couples

18.8%

18.4%

17.9%

12.4%

7.6%

7.6%

5.8%

8.5%

8.1%

4.3%

3.1%

2.0%

Source: LGBTmap.org

their amended versions of the YRBS, but these locales are the exception not the rule.

The lack of comprehensive research about LGBT YOC, and to a lesser extent LGBT youth, means that the knowledge professionals working with LGBT YOC have is anecdotal or qualitative in nature. For LGBT YOC advocates, the research gaps on LGBT YOC present a credibility challenge during attempts to raise the public's awareness of the obstacles confronting this vulnerable population. With a paucity in peer-reviewed data to understand the unique experience of LGBT YOC, one has to make certain assumptions about the challenges and experiences of LGBT YOC based on information about LGBT youth and data on general population YOC.

Poverty

There may be more LGBT-identified youth, and potentially LGBT YOC, living in poverty now than at any point in US history. There are an estimated 60-70 million young people in the US between ages five and twenty, a youth population explosion not recorded in the US since the baby boom generation. Of these youth, one in three are a member of a racial or ethnic minority. Social scientists generally estimate that 10% of youth are or will become lesbian, gay, bisexual or transgender. The 2000 Census reports that youth under 18 comprise the largest number of people living in poverty in the US, and youth 18 to 24 had a poverty rate of 14.4%. Employer discrimination against youth based on age (which contributes to low youth wages and the income disparities between old and young workers); youth unemployment that can be as high as 33% in some cities; and government-sanctioned employment discrimination in 40 states against self-identified LGBT populations ensure that LGBT youth and young adults are well represented among communities of poor and working-class people. LGBT YOC, particularly those of African-American, Native American and Latino descent may be disproportionately represented among LGBT youth living in poverty, given the high poverty rates for those communities, the disproportionately low wages paid to these workers, and the potential for racial discrimination in hiring and job promotion.

[…]

Racial, Ethnic and Cultural Concerns Facing LGBT YOC

LGBT YOC who come out in their racial or ethnic communities risk separation from their cultural communities and the loss of support for their racial and ethnic identities. The individualism often espoused by the framers of a Westernized gay identity, which often is a consequence of that identity, is often considered by communities of color to be antithetical to the interdependent communal and family relationships traditionally promoted by those communities. Through these interdependent family and communal structures, cultural expectations and determinants of cultural "authenticity" are defined and reinforced. Cultural expectation of and adherence to strict gender roles are also developed within the contexts of this communal framework. Such expectations may include machismo and sexual prowess in Latino, African American and Filipino males. In some Latino and API communities, these cultural markers often allow same sex behavior by men as long as these men discreetly engage in these behaviors, adhere to strict gender roles, and meet their family's expectations of marriage and reproduction.

Affirmed expressions of gender variance and open sexual liberation often found in the politicized gay, lesbian and transgendered identities in the US are viewed by many communities of color as a threat to the patriarchal family structure and the interdependent nature of their communities. This view holds particularly true for newly immigrated people of color and others who exhibit low levels of acculturation and place a premium on males and masculine behavior. Religious beliefs, like Islam, that condemn homosexuality and further determine the cultural norms and mores of communities of color reinforce resistance to acknowledging and affirming LGBT identities.

Despite evidence to the contrary, members of communities of color often see LGBT identities as "white identities" and declarations of an LGBT identity as a rejection of communities of color values and traditions. Communities of color are in denial about ethnographic studies that document known and occasionally celebrated instances of homosexuality and transgendered behavior in their pre-colonization histories. For example, men in some pre-colonial African tribes engaged in homosexual acts as a norm during an adolescent male's rites of passage into adulthood, and some Native American and Filipino cultures believed in a "third sex," those whose behavior seemed to embody both the masculine and the feminine, and placed those who exhibited this gender variance in a high place of esteem. Rather than accept a range of human sexuality and gender expression within their communities' culture and histories, communities of color often ostracize LGBT YOC who disclose their orientation, refuse to adhere to a cultural code of silence on sexuality, and/or are unable to comfortably fit the gender roles. Since these communities often are the only affirming constructs of a youth's cultural, racial, and/or religious identity, LGBT YOC often lack cultural support.

[...]

Conclusion

Despite LGBT YOC's membership in groups with an increased probability of risk for developing chronic and costly conditions, the current public health system is largely hostile to or uniformed about their needs. Without significant system-wide reform and a healthy dose of tolerance, LGBT YOC will continue to exhibit high rates of preventable disease and poor health outcomes.

Similarly, the range of child protective services frequently fail LGBT youth and LGBT YOC with their propensity to engage in implicit denial of the challenges LGBT youth experience in foster care and group home settings and these services' explicit refusal to acknowledge the existence of these populations in their care. The lack of cultural and social support structures for youth to meet their developmental needs are too often denied to LGBT YOC, and the few resources available to LGBT YOC too often demand that these young people compartmentalize and prioritize their multiple identities and oppressions. Society sets up LGBT YOC for failure through institutional, economic and cultural oppression rooted in heterosexism, homophobia and transphobia. This societal and institutional failure is compounded by the additional challenges LGBT YOC confront in being a racial or ethnic minority.

To improve the health and developmental outcomes for LGBT YOC, more research is needed to determine the needs and address the health status of this population; there need to be more GSAs and safe school coalitions working in schools and districts with a high concentration of racial and ethnic minorities; cultural competency education is needed for LGBT CBO's working with LGBT YOC; targeted sexuality education and tolerance initiatives that address the homophobia and heterosexism culturally rooted in minority communities need to be developed and implemented; LGBT youth sensitivity protocols for professionals working in the child welfare and juvenile justice system must be created, and societal tolerance must be increased.

Until society is able to scrutinize the values, systems and practices that create the oppressive conditions and poor life outcomes experienced by those whose lives and being defy simplistic categorization, LGBT YOC will continue to be the most underserved and vulnerable population of any youth population in the United States.

FIVE

LGBTQ Teens Are at Risk for Homelessness for Many Reasons

Center for American Progress

LGBTQ teens face higher rates of abuse and victimization, family rejection and discrimination leading to personal and social problems, and harassment at school leading to higher dropout rates. In the following viewpoint, the Center for American Progress explains that a disproportionate number of the more than two million homeless youth in the US are gay, lesbian, bisexual, transgender, or queer. Many leave home due to family conflict and encounter discrimination when seeking shelter. This discrimination is also prevalent in federally funded programs. According to the authors, Congress has the responsibility to make a financial commitment to direct services for these young people. The Center for American Progress is a progressive public policy research and advocacy organization.

There are approximately 1.6 million to 2.8 million homeless young people in the United States, and estimates suggest that disproportionate numbers of those youth are gay, lesbian, bisexual, or transgender. These vulnerable gay and transgender youth often run away from home because of family conflict and then face overt discrimination when seeking alternative housing, which is compounded by institutionalized discrimination in federally funded programs.

"Gay and Transgender Youth Homelessness by the Numbers," Center for American Progress, June 21, 2010. Reprinted by permission.

LGBTQ teens are at high risk of being abused and victimized.

We do not have to accept this reality. The federal government has the power to reduce and eventually eliminate rates of gay and transgender youth homelessness while addressing youth homelessness overall. Congress can and should make a financial commitment to services directed at these young people. They should join with federal agencies and couple it with an expansion of equal rights and protections to all gay, lesbian, bisexual, and transgender people. As the numbers below show, it's time we provide these young people with the help they need.

An alarming number of gay and transgender young people are homeless

- 1.6 million to 2.8 million: The estimated number of homeless youth in the United States.

- 20 to 40 percent: The portion of the homeless youth population who are gay or transgender, compared to only 5 to 10 percent of the overall youth population.

- 320,000 to 400,000: A conservative estimate of the number of gay and transgender youth facing homelessness each year.

- 14.4: The average age that lesbian and gay youth in New York become homeless.

- 13.5: The average age that transgender youth in New York become homeless

Homeless gay and transgender youth see higher rates of abuse and victimization

- 58 percent: The portion of homeless gay and transgender youth who have been sexually assaulted, compared to 33 percent of homeless heterosexual youth.

- 44 percent: The portion of homeless gay and transgender youth who reported being asked by someone on the street to exchange sex for money, food, drugs, shelter, or clothes, compared to 26 percent of straight homeless youth.

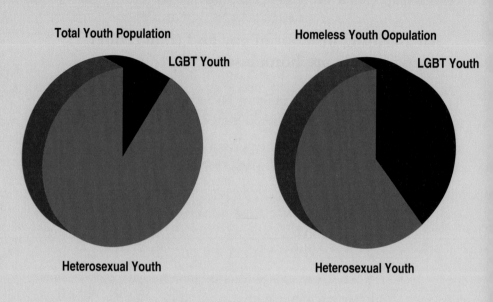

Percentage of total US youth population that identifies as LGBT versus percentage of US homeless youth population that identifies as LGBT

Total Youth Population

LGBT Youth

Heterosexual Youth

Homeless Youth Oopulation

LGBT Youth

Heterosexual Youth

Source: Center for American Progress

Rejection and discrimination at home lead to severe personal and social problems

- 13: The average age gay and lesbian youth now come out after self-identifying as gay or lesbian as young as ages 5 to 7.

- 62 percent: The portion of homeless gay and transgender youth who experience discrimination from their families, compared to 30 percent of their heterosexual peers.

- 42 percent: The portion of homeless gay and transgender youth who abuse alcohol, compared to 27 percent of heterosexual youth.

- 62 percent: The portion of homeless gay and transgender youth who attempt suicide, compared to 29 percent of their heterosexual homeless peers.

- 8.4 times: How much more likely gay and transgender youth are to attempt suicide if they are rejected by their families in adolescence compared to if they are not rejected by their family. They are also 5.9 times as likely to have experienced depression, 3.4 times as likely to have used illicit drugs, and 3.4 times as likely to have had unprotected sex.

Harassment at school leads to high dropout rates

- 86 percent: The portion of gay and lesbian students who reported being verbally harassed at school due to their sexual orientation in 2007.

- 44 percent: The portion of gay and lesbian students who reported being physically harassed at school because of their sexual orientation in 2007.

- 22 percent: The portion of gay and transgender students who reported having been physically attacked in school in 2007. Sixty percent say they did not report the incidents because they believed no one would care.

- 31 percent: The portion of gay and transgender students who report incidents of harassment and violence at school to staff only to receive no response.

- Two times: How much less likely gay and transgender students are to finish high school or pursue a college education compared to the national average.

Child welfare systems often fail to protect gay and transgender youth

- 78 percent: The portion of gay and transgender youth who were either removed from or ran away from their New York foster care placements due to conflict and discrimination related to their sexual orientation or gender identity.

- 88 percent: The portion of professional staff in out-of-home placements who say that gay and transgender youth were not safe in group-home environments.

- $53,665: The estimated cost to maintain a youth in the criminal justice system for one year, while it only costs $5,887 to permanently move a homeless youth off the streets and prevent them from reentering the criminal justice system.

Federal programs overlook homeless gay and transgender youth

- $195 million: The portion of the federal government's $4.2 billion budget for homeless-assistance programs that is targeted toward homeless youth.

- Less than 1 percent: The portion of the $44 billion federal budget for rental assistance, public housing, and affordable housing programs allocated for homeless youth housing assistance.

- 44,483: The number of youth who were given a bed in a shelter through Runaway and Homeless Youth Act programs in 2008, compared to 766,800 homeless youth identified through these programs.

SIX

Homeless Teens Are a Problem in Every Region of the World

The International Child and Youth Care Network

Teens living on the streets are especially vulnerable to victimization, exploitation, and the abuse of their civil and economic rights. In the following viewpoint the International Child and Youth Care Network argues that indifference to the problem has led to continual neglect and abuse of these youth. Girls also have a greater vulnerability to trafficking for commercial sexual exploitation or other forms of child labor. Many homeless teens are enticed by adults and older youths into selling drugs, stealing, and prostitution. Drug use by teens on the streets is common as they look for ways to numb the pain. The International Child and Youth Care Network is a South Africa-based organization for professionals who work with troubled youth.

Street Children Facts

- There are an estimated 100 million children living in the streets in the world today.
- Children living on the streets are especially vulnerable to victimization, exploitation, and the abuse of their civil and economic rights.

"Street children and homelessness," edited by Amod K. Kanth, Prayas Juvenile Aid Centre Society and Bruce Harris, Casa Alianza, The International Child and Youth Care Network, Issue 68, September 2004. Reprinted by permission.

- International indifference to the problem has led to continual neglect and abuse of these children.

Who Are Considered Homeless and Street Children?

Article 27 of the Convention on the Rights of the Child (CRC) asserts that "States Parties recognize the right of every child to a standard of living adequate for the child's physical, mental, spiritual, moral and social development." Homelessness denies each one of those rights. According to an Inter-NGO Program on street children and youth, a street child is "any girl or boy who has not reached adulthood, for whom the street (in the widest sense of the word, including unoccupied dwellings, wasteland, etc.) has become his or her habitual abode and/or source of livelihood, and who is inadequately protected, directed, and supervised by responsible adults."

USAID has divided Street Children into Four Categories:

- A 'Child of the Streets': Children who have no home but the streets, and no family support. They move from place to place, living in shelters and abandoned buildings.

- A 'Child on the street': Children who visit their families regularly and might even return every night to sleep at home, but spend most days and some nights on the street because of poverty, overcrowding, sexual or physical abuse at home.

- Part of a Street Family: These children live on sidewalks or city squares with the rest of their families. They may be displaced due to poverty, wars, or natural disasters. The families often live a nomadic life, carrying their possessions with them. Children in this case often work on the streets with other members of their families.

- In Institutionalized Care: Children in this situation come from a situation of homelessness and are at risk of returning to a life on the street.

Travel around the world's greatest cities and you will see teens living on the street. How can this problem be solved?

Street Child Statistics

The hidden and isolated nature of street children makes accurate statistics difficult to gather; however, UNICEF estimates there are approximately 100 million street children worldwide with that number constantly growing. There are up to 40 million street children in Latin America, and at least 18 million in India.[1] Many studies have determined that street children are most often boys aged 10 to 14, with increasingly younger children being affected (Amnesty International, 1999).[2] Many girls live on the streets as well,[3] although smaller numbers are reported due to their being

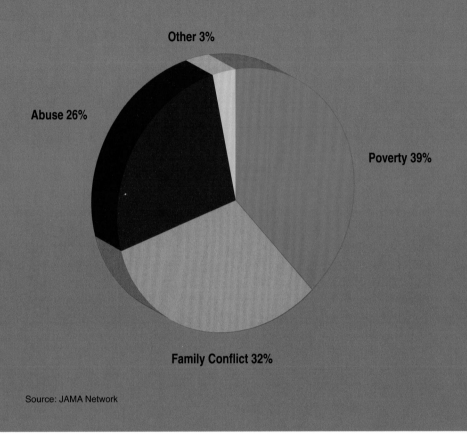

Main reported reasons for homelessness among youths ages twenty-four and younger, globally

Other 3%

Abuse 26%

Poverty 39%

Family Conflict 32%

Source: JAMA Network

more "useful" in the home, taking care of younger siblings and cooking. Girls also have a greater vulnerability to trafficking for commercial sexual exploitation or other forms of child labor.

Where Do Homeless and Street Children Live Around the World

Homelessness is largely an urban phenomenon, yet children are homeless and living on the streets in every region of the world from developing countries to the most affluent countries. Latin America and India, for example, are known for their large populations of street children,[4] despite the significant efforts of some governments and non-governmental organizations. The AIDS epidemic and civil wars in Africa have caused a surge in the number of street children as a result of the abandonment of AIDS orphans or fatalities due to armed conflict. Failing economies and falling currencies in parts of Asia force the poorest families onto the street, often leaving children abandoned and homeless. Unstable political transitions, such as the end of Communism in Eastern Europe , caused unprecedented numbers of street children due to inadequate social security for the poor and those formerly State supported. Children often experience the effects of political, economic, and social crises within their countries more severely than adults, and many lack the adequate institutional support to address their special needs. Eventually, they end up on the streets.

Perspective: In 1996, the United States had 5.5 million children living in extreme poverty, approximately one million of whom were on the streets.[5] A study conducted by the Luxembourg Income Study shows poor children in the United States are poorer than children in most Western industrialized countries, since the United States has less generous social programs, the widest gap between rich and poor, and high numbers of poor immigrant and unwed teen mothers.[6] The poverty and social conditions many American children face lead to large numbers of homeless and street children.

Vulnerability and Homeless and Street Children

Children who are vulnerable to street life include those who have been abandoned by their families or sent into cities because of a family's intense poverty, often with hopes that a child will be able to earn money for the family and send it home. Children who run away from home or children's institutions frequently end up on the street since they rarely return home due to dysfunctional families, or physical, mental, and/or sexual abuse. In several areas of the world, disabled children are commonly abandoned, particularly in developing countries. In addition, refugee children of armed conflict areas, children separated from their families for long periods of time, and AIDS orphans, repeatedly find nowhere to go but the streets.

The Effects of Street and Homeless life

Homelessness and street life have extremely detrimental effects on children. Their unstable lifestyles, lack of medical care, and inadequate living conditions increase young people's susceptibility to chronic illnesses such as respiratory or ear infections, gastrointestinal disorders, and sexually-transmitted diseases, including HIV/AIDS.[7] Children fending for themselves must find ways to eat; some scavenge or find exploitative physical work. Many homeless children are enticed by adults and older youth into selling drugs, stealing, and prostitution.

Drug use by children on the streets is common as they look for means to numb the pain and deal with the hardships associated with street life. Studies have found that up to 90 percent of street children use psychoactive substances, including medicines, alcohol, cigarettes, heroin, cannabis, and readily available industrial products such as shoe glue.

The mental, social and emotional growth of children are affected by their nomadic lifestyles and the way in which they are chastised by authorities who constantly expel them from their temporary homes such as doorways, park benches, and railway platforms. Countries in Latin America like Colombia, Guatemala, Honduras, and Brazil are notorious for the torture and violence inflicted on street children, many times escalating to murder — by police officers or death squads. Street children lack security, protection, and hope, and continue to face a deep-rooted negative stigma about homelessness. And, more than anything else, they lack love.

Protecting Children

Many governments, nongovernmental organizations, and members of civil society around the world have increased their attention on homeless and street children as the number of this disenfranchised population continues to grow dramatically. Nonetheless, more action is necessary. Most importantly, as a result of adverse economic conditions in many countries, an international plan to provide basic housing needs to be developed.

In 1992, the United Nations issued a Resolution on the Plight of Street Children, expressing concern over the emergence and marginalization of street children, and the acts of violence against them. The Resolution called for international cooperation to address the needs of homeless children and for enforcement of international child rights laws. European nations that have taken effective steps toward combating homelessness include Belgium, Finland, the Netherlands, Portugal, and Spain. In many countries, governments have included a right to housing in the national constitution.[8] The Finnish devised a plan in 1987 including house-building, social welfare, health care service, and a duty to provide a decent home for every homeless person. The number of homeless people in Finland was cut in half after 10 years.[9] However, the major problem with State programs is that children often reject the alternative assistance offered by the State.

On a local and regional level, initiatives have been taken to assist street children, often through shelters. Many shelters have programs designed to provide safety, healthcare, counseling, education, vocational training, legal aid, and other social services. Some shelters also provide regular individual contact, offering much-needed love and care.

Many NGOs have been founded with mission to improve the plight of homeless adults and youth. Casa Alianza, active in Mexico and Central America; Child Hope UK working with local groups worldwide; Butterflies, based in New Delhi, India; and, Street Kids International, a Canadian-based organization, all focus specifically on street children. Prayas Juvenile Aid Centre (JAC) Society, based in Delhi, India , pioneered the first intensive study on Homeless children ever conducted; they have also set up numerous shelters providing basic security, food, and clothing for more than 50,000 homeless people in Greater Delhi.

Get Involved

If you are interested in helping street and homeless children, you can volunteer to work in shelters and other programs in your area, or donate funds or supplies to organizations that work with street youth. You can also participate in legislative efforts and write letters to your Congressional Representative urging him/her to support increased funding for programs in the United States and abroad that assist street children. Finally, you can raise awareness of this issue by educating yourself, your peers, colleagues, students, teachers, family members, and others around you interested in this issue.

Notes

1 http://www.oneworld.org/guides/streetchildren/

2 Beasley, Rob. "On the Streets," *Amnesty Magazine*. April 1999.

3 Ibid.

4 Ibid.

5 Alston, Philip. "Hardship in the Midst of Plenty," *The Progress of Nations* , 1998, p. 29.

6 "U.S. Poor are among World's Poorest," *The New York Times* , August 14, 1999 .

7 Alston, Philip. P. 29.

8 Ibid. p. 31.

9 Ibid.

SEVEN

Mentally Ill Teens Need Special Care and Treatment

Sam P. K. Collins

Along with the more basic needs, homeless teens struggle with emotional and mental stress at higher rates than others in their age group. In the following viewpoint, Sam P.K. Collins explains that homeless youth are at a much greater risk of developmental delays, social and emotional problems, and problems at school. Lack of stable housing, lack of sleep, hunger, and fear can increase the production of cortisol, a stress hormone that alters young brains, during their developmental period. The unaddressed physical and mental abuse that may have taken place during the period of homelessness can devastate them later in life. Collins is a journalist and educator based in Washington, DC.

Life in a shelter, exposure to violence, poverty, and inadequate health care all take a toll on homeless children—putting them in greater need of mental health services compared to their counterparts who live in more stable environments, a new study has confirmed.

Researchers at North Carolina State University compiled data on more than homeless 300 children between the ages of 2 months to 6 years who lived in 11 Wake County, NC-based shelters. Their long-term study found that 25 percent of the youngsters needed

The stressful conditions homeless teens face put them in greater need of mental health services.

mental health services. These findings came on the heels of other reports that showed linkages between homelessness and well below academic and language skills for 5 and 6 year-olds.

"As a result of their exposure to those difficult life circumstances—combined with living in a shelter—homeless children are at a much greater risk of developmental delays, social and emotional problems, and problems at school," Jenna Armstrong, co-author of the study and Ph.D. candidate at the university, told MedicineNet.com. "[T]he scale of the problem is huge."

A Growing Problem

Nearly 2.5 million children end up homeless in the United States, according to data collected by the National Center on Family Homelessness. In 2013, the homeless child population reached historic highs with youngsters in urban centers and rural areas of the United States finding "shelter" in the streets, in cars, campgrounds, or with family members in tight quarters for a short amount of time.

The above-average increase—more than 8 percentage points—in the homeless child population stems from government policies that have overlooked families, even while taking steps in connecting chronically homeless individuals and veterans with shelter. A significant number of homeless families are headed by single women who are victims of violence, one-third of whom have developed post-traumatic stress disorder. More than half of the women in these situations have depressive episodes while caring for their young children.

For children living in these situations, lack of stable housing, lack of sleep, hunger, and fear can increase the production of cortisol, a stress hormone that alters young brains, during the developmental period of their lives. Homeless youth between the ages of 6 and 17 struggle with anxiety, depression, and withdrawal at a rate nearly 30 percentage points higher than other children in that age group. In school, homeless youth are four times as likely to have developmental delays in their speech, cognition, and social and motor skills. They also stand a greater chance of developing learning disabilities and repeating a grade because of extended absences, frequent school transfers, and lack of transportation. One in four homeless children also reported eating less.

"We like to believe that education the great equalizer in our society. As long as you try hard you'll have a chance to improve your situation but if you're spending your night in a tent or in a car how are you going to succeed in school?" Rachael Myers, executive director of the Washington Low Income Housing Alliance, told a Washington state NBC affiliate. Myers is supporting a state bill that would provide affordable housing and other services to families dealing with homelessness and mental health issues that make it difficult for children to consistently attend school. With stalled education funding, however, the bill may not pass.

More than likely, school is the last thing on the minds of a growing number of young people who are facing homelessness

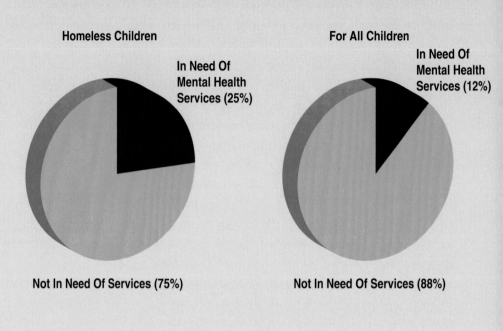

Percentage of homeless children in need of mental health services versus percentage of all children in need of services

Homeless Children

In Need Of Mental Health Services (25%)

Not In Need Of Services (75%)

For All Children

In Need Of Mental Health Services (12%)

Not In Need Of Services (88%)

Source: North Carolina State University via MedicineNet

alone. For example, children transitioning into adulthood after stints in foster care report being homeless at least once, according to data compiled by Chapin Hall at the University of Chicago. Research has shown that history of physical abuse and delinquent behavior that developed as a result of trauma counts among the key causes of homelessness among foster children, struggling to find their way without a concrete plan for housing and financial assets.

Identifying the Risks

In recent years, more LGBT children—a group that accounts for more than 30 percent of the homeless youth population—have found themselves on the streets after coming out to their family. Homeless LBGT youth have a greater risk of social stigma and discrimination because of their sexual orientation. They're turned away from homeless shelters at a rate greater than that of their peers. Transgender youth, in particular, have a greater chance of experiencing physical harm, abuse, and exploitation on the streets and in shelters, factors that make them more likely to become depressed.

"Prevention and early intervention is the way to go," David Murphey, a senior research fellow at the Child Trends research center, told The Youth Project, a media outlet that address public policy issues affecting youth, in 2013. "Taking a pro-active approach could prevent things for getting worse later, he said, encouraging listeners to learn the tell-tale signs of common disorders, speak out if they notice any, and extend help to young people who look as if they need a hand. Treatment that combines talk therapy with medication has been shown to be most effective, he said.

No matter the circumstance, the unaddressed physical and mental abuse that may have taken place during the period of homelessness can devastate children later in life. Homeless youth stand a greater chance of abusing substances, attempting suicide, participating in criminal activity, and most importantly becoming homeless later in adulthood.

The Centers for Disease Control and Prevention says that parent and school administrators—people who are in contact with children for up to one-third of the day—play a unique role in recognizing the telltale signs of mental illness and connecting children with mental health care. In 2010, the U.S. Interagency Council on Homelessness adopted the Framework to End Youth Homelessness, an approach that proponents said will provide stable housing, education, and social-welling programs for homeless youth.

"In contrast to common perceptions, homelessness is not just an adult phenomenon; youth are resorting to abandoned buildings, park benches, makeshift shelters, and staying with friends and sometimes strangers," the U.S. Interagency Council on

Homelessness wrote in the introduction of its 2013 report about the trauma of youth homelessness.

"Many of these youth have experienced significant trauma before and after becoming homeless. Often they face struggles across multiple aspects of daily life that contribute to their vulnerability," the report continues. "At the same time, all youth have strengths, but youth experiencing homelessness often lack positive opportunities and supports to apply them. An effective strategy must account for the specific needs of adolescents and youth transitioning to adulthood and the role families can play in both the reasons for becoming homeless and the potential solutions."

EIGHT

It Is an Educator's Responsibility to Help Homeless Teens

Mark Keierleber

> In the following excerpted viewpoint Mark Keierleber explains how school administrators and educators can help assure that homeless teens achieve academic success. There are many challenges faced by students when they call a shelter home, and education often gets pushed to the side. Support for students living in shelters is woefully inadequate and bureaucratically entangled. Federal law requires schools to hire liaisons to identify and help address student homelessness, but there is a lack of coordination between city housing and education agencies, inadequate school funding to combat homelessness, and a lack of trained officials to deal with student needs. Keierleber is a journalist at The 74.

The little apartment around the corner from the Utica Avenue subway stop wasn't much, but it was theirs. Darius Hansome got the one bedroom, while his mother, Traci, slept in the living room.

Then gentrification arrived in their central Brooklyn neighborhood of Crown Heights, most widely known for years for the deadly riots that erupted in 1991 between the area's African-American and Orthodox Jewish residents.

The lingering stain from that violence was swept away by new,

"The Homeless Student Population Is Exploding. Will New Focus on Performance Save Them?" by Mark Keierleber, The 74 Media, Inc., October 16, 2016. The74million.org. Reprinted by permission.

Teens who live in homeless shelters do have a chance at academic success.

hip coffee shops, pricey bars and a mob of white, younger residents staking claim to the freshly renovated pre-war apartments and the new luxury buildings towering over the crummy bodegas and liquor stores.

Crown Heights acquired cachet so quickly that longtime residents, like Darius and his mom, could not keep up. In the summer of 2013, their landlord emptied nearly their entire building, save for only a few tenants. Some of the renters were price-gouged, Traci said, while others were bought out.

And some, like Traci and her son, were left homeless. Traci, 38, a home health aide out of work because of a chronic medical issue, fought for months to keep their apartment, but a few weeks before Christmas, in the middle of Darius's freshman year of high school, she lost.

Darius longs for that small apartment in Crown Heights. He had his own bedroom. He could shut the door for privacy. And he had Rōnin, the stray kitten he begged his mother to adopt.

Today, Darius has none of those things. He and his mother live in a family homeless shelter in East New York, where they hesitate to crack open a window because a thick, rancid chemical smell seeps in from nearby car detailing shops. Darius wants to become a writer, a novelist in fact, but the small studio apartment isn't conducive to creativity, he said. It's also not a great place to complete homework.

"It's altered my perspective on life," Darius said about having no place to live. "I mean, you never know what you have until it's gone, to put that simply, and I hate to use a cliché."

Homeless in High School

Darius has spent nearly his entire high school career living in a homeless shelter, just one young man among more than a million homeless students in the U.S., a population that's been largely invisible in American education policy talks. But in acknowledgment of a deep vulnerability — from chronic absenteeism to staggering high school dropout rates — lawmakers are now placing a fresh emphasis on tracking and improving the outcomes of displaced students through the new federal education law, the Every Student Succeeds Act.

Nowhere is this effort more concentrated than in New York City, where the homeless student population has exploded in the past decade to more than 80,000 and where local officials are scrambling to educate them. Yet a city study released just last week acknowledged these efforts are far too little.

Last month, Darius started his senior year at Park Slope Collegiate, a public school that he calls a "hell hole," where the metal detectors at the front door offer "an illusion of safety." In a matter of months, the 17-year-old, whose cynicism starts to crack when he talks about his writing or about his favorite video games, is expected to graduate and to attend college — a remarkable feat for a young man without a permanent home.

For Darius, getting this far in school wasn't easy. The boy is "academically lazy," his mother observes sharply, and his grades from the past school year show it. He doesn't like school, but he knows the only way out is to finish. Helping him reach the graduation stage are a doggedly determined mother (Traci sent a younger Darius to live with relatives in Hawaii because she was so distraught over the schools in Jamaica, Queens), supportive teachers and a fraternity of Brooklyn teenagers who've had similar experiences whom Darius met through a city Department of Education program.

That's more than a lot of homeless students in New York City — or many other places in the country — can claim.

The just-released report — "Not Reaching the Door: Homeless Students Face Many Hurdles on the Way to School" — from the city's Independent Budget Office highlights the many challenges students face when they call a shelter home. Supports for students living in shelters — more than a third of all the temporarily housed students in 2013–14, the year studied — are woefully inadequate and bureaucratically entangled, the report found.

The author highlighted a lack of coordination between city housing and education agencies, inadequate school funding to combat homelessness, and a lack of trained officials to deal with student needs.

Federal law requires schools to hire liaisons to identify and help address student homelessness, but the report found that the city Department of Education was "short-staffed" to handle a population that is rapidly multiplying. The city employs 10 people who

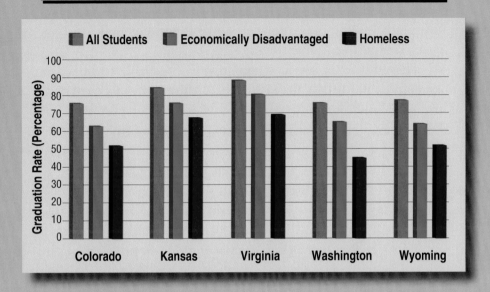

Graduation rates among homeless, economically disadvantaged, and total students in five states, class of 2014

■ All Students　　■ Economically Disadvantaged　　■ Homeless

Graduation Rate (Percentage)

Colorado　Kansas　Virginia　Washington　Wyoming

Source: Civic Enterprises

oversee 32 community districts and more than 100 shelter-based liaisons charged with making sure children get to school.

For the homeless kids who make up those overwhelming case-loads, life's struggles are compounded.

"I think what stands out is the fact that students in tempo-rary housing situations deal with all of these factors together," said Liza Pappas, an education policy and budget analyst at the Independent Budget Office, who wrote the report. "So challenges going to school, the trauma of living in a homeless shelter, not having adequate resources."

Tracking Homeless Students for the First Time

Homelessness has a profound effect on student performance, yet schools often struggle to identify displaced students and to offer them the supports they need.

In most states, including New York, school districts aren't required to report the graduation rates of students experiencing homelessness.

Of the five states that currently do report graduation rates for homeless youth — Colorado, Kansas, Virginia, Washington and Wyoming — data show displaced students perform far below their peers, trailing even other low-income students.

The amount of services and supports available to homeless students varies widely between school districts across the country, said Erin Ingram, a co-author of a recent report by Civic Enterprises, "Hidden in Plain Sight," which explored the barriers homeless youth face in their efforts to graduate. While some schools offer resources ranging from help in finding housing to flexible academic requirements, that's not a universal experience.

"We also heard from some students who said, 'You know, I told people I was homeless, and nothing was done for me,'" Ingram said.

That's beginning to change. Starting this month, school districts across the country are being asked to do more for their homeless student population.

Under the Every Student Succeeds Act, schools are required to hire personnel who are adequately prepared to help homeless students achieve. States are required to allocate more federal money to district efforts to educate homeless children. And by next year, all states will be required to report the graduation rates of students experiencing homelessness, in the same way they do other vulnerable groups, such as the disabled and English-language learners.

Ingram hopes this new set of numbers will help educators target the students having the greatest difficulties.

"We know this is a group of kids who really need a lot of support and deserve a lot of focus," Ingram said. "We're really hopeful that just getting that data can give us a better sense of which kids are in need of a lot of supports."

[…]

More Homeless Students than Seattle, Boston Combined

Though student homelessness is expected in New York City, it still remains largely an invisible epidemic because students feel the stigma and parents fear they could lose custody of their children if their status were known.

Nationally, homelessness has nearly doubled in American public schools since the 2006–07 school year, affecting more than 1.3 million students in 2013–14. Minority and LGBT students are disproportionately represented in this population. Often, people think homelessness "is something that happens somewhere else, in someone else's neighborhood," particularly in large cities like New York and San Francisco, Ingram said. But that's not so.

"This is part of our national picture, particularly because we think the Great Recession pushed so many families out of their housing," she said. "A lot of those families still have not regained stability."

In New York City, where 1.1 million children are enrolled in public schools, one in eight students has experienced homelessness within the past five years. That's 127,000 kids — more students than the Boston and Seattle school districts combined.

Earlier this year, New York City Mayor Bill de Blasio announced that the city would spend $30 million on services to address the homeless student population, using the money to establish health centers at elementary schools, launch literacy programs in homeless shelters and hire attendance specialists and social workers. The move followed cries from critics who said his administration was doing too little.

"Students in temporary housing are among our most vulnerable populations," Toya Holness, a city education department spokeswoman, said in a statement responding to the Independent Budget Office's findings. "We are working across city agencies to implement these critical programs and provide supports to families to ensure students living in temporary housing receive an equitable and excellent education."

NINE

Target the Psychosocial Barriers to Homeless Teens' Succcess

Tori DeAngelis

> At-risk students need extra help in order to succeed, and that is especially true for homeless students. In the following viewpoint, Tori DeAngelis reports on a program that supports learning among at-risk students. This program targets the barriers—psychological, educational, and social—that prevent such students from achieving their full potential. Although the program was started at UCLA, it is being implemented in several states across the country. The hope is that this holistic approach focusing on the whole child, not just academics, will be a success in impoverished school systems and beyond. DeAngelis is a writer in Syracuse, N.Y.

In 2003, Sabine Parish—a poor, low-performing school district in rural Louisiana—hired Dorman Jackson as superintendent because of his reputation for raising test scores. He instituted a remedial-learning program to catch and treat learning problems early, and soon, students' academic performance started to rise.

But at a certain point, that trajectory halted. "We discovered we had carried our kids about as far as we could," says Jackson.

After speaking with the district's student assessment and support services department, he learned more about why: Many

There are so many barriers that keep homeless teens from achiev-
ing their potential. School programs dedicated to at-risk students
have met with success.

of these students faced significant personal roadblocks that prevented them from doing well in school, including overworked or
absent parents, emotional problems, and drug and alcohol abuse.

That's when Jackson's staff suggested that the school work
with psychologists Howard Adelman, PhD, and Linda Taylor, PhD,
who co-direct the University of California, Los Angeles, School
Mental Health Project and the federally funded National Center
for Mental Health in Schools. They had developed a model called
"the enabling component"—also referred to as "learning supports"

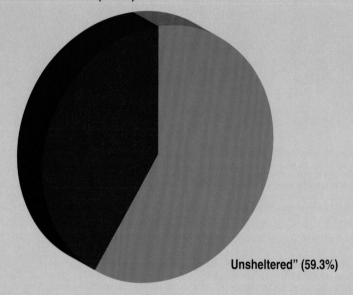

Percentage of unaccompanied homeless minors (ages eighteen and under) that were unsheltered, January 2014

Staying in a Homeless Shelter (40.7%)

Unsheltered" (59.3%)

Source: U.S. Department of Housing and Urban Development

by schools, districts and other entities that implement it. It targets the psychosocial and educational barriers to student success.

The model does that in two ways. First, it aims to consolidate and coordinate student and learning supports—the counseling services, school prevention and intervention programs, and community resources that tend to be fragmented and uncoordinated at many schools. Second, the model offers interventions to address barriers to learning and teaching, such as bringing support staff directly into the classroom to work with kids, and making better connections with and use of community resources to help struggling children and their families.

The approach appears to be working in Sabine Parish: From 2007 and 2010, graduation rates rose from 73 percent to 81.2 percent. In addition, of the state's 60 districts, Sabine has gone from 37th in 2003 to 14th this year in academic performance.

Jackson doesn't think the school could have gotten there without the psychological and social support the enabling component model provided. "I have appreciated gaining the knowledge that when a kid is having a problem in their family or with themselves," Jackson says, "they're not going to be successful unless you fix that problem."

Now, the UCLA team is taking its work nationwide, holding forums for educational and policy leaders in 13 states and helping implement the program at the state, district and school levels.

How the Model Works

Adelman and Taylor's enabling component model was developed after 30 years of research and observation in their lab school at UCLA and in the Los Angeles public schools. Through their work, Adelman and Taylor observed two trends. For one, they saw that pulling at-risk students out of class to be counseled, punished or suspended for aggressive behaviors or bullying interfered with their peer relationships and academic progress. The psychologists discovered that keeping these children in stimulating, supportive classrooms helped them to stop acting out, learn and share their own unique gifts with other kids.

Second, Adelman and Taylor noticed an enormous redundancy in schools' mental health and social services. When they developed a program to prevent school dropout, for instance, "we soon realized that at some school sites, we were one of 15 similar programs that were trying to address risky behaviors," Taylor says.

As they continued to see these phenomena play out in school and after school, it became clear the system needed an overhaul, Adelman says. "We thought there had to be a way to bring all of this together—not just to coordinate programs, but to really develop a major intervention framework," he says.

Their "enabling component" encourages school action in six areas:

1. **Making innovative changes to classroom instruction.** That includes bringing support personnel into the classroom, rather than taking children out of class when their behavior or inattention may have gotten out of control. It also calls for revamping teaching and intervention methods to help teachers handle problems more easily and effectively.

2. **Supporting children through transitions.** Not only are children moving back and forth from school to home and from one school level to the next, many are also coping with family disruptions, such as a divorce.

3. **Connecting families to schools and school activities.** This includes offering basic parenting classes, fostering more meetings between parents and teachers and involving families in homework projects, field trips and other activities.

4. **Maximizing use of community resources.** Developing and maintaining strong connections with community resources can greatly enhance schools' capacity to support these youngsters. Entities to tap include public and private agencies, colleges and universities, businesses, artists and cultural institutions, faith-based organizations and volunteer groups.

5. **Reorganizing crisis assistance and prevention.** Schools need systems that can respond quickly and effectively in the wake of any crisis, whether it is a natural disaster, a terrorist attack or student acting in a way that endangers others. Schools must also create safe and caring learning environments that deal preemptively with disruptive and potentially dangerous behavior such as bullying and harassment.

6. **Improving links to external mental health and behavioral services.** When internal resources aren't enough, schools should be able to refer students and families

to mental health and financial assistance services in a timely fashion.

The framework also emphasizes the need to build students' sense of competence, self-determination and connections with others, rather than punishing them for "bad" behavior, says Taylor. "It's a new way of thinking about how to deal with at-risk kids so they really feel like school is the place for them, rather than a place to avoid," she says.

In this era of belt-tightening, the model may also save schools money by streamlining services and using resources more effectively, Adelman adds.

Growing Support

Several states are implementing the model in ways tailored to their circumstances, budget and needs. In Iowa, the learning supports model is being embedded in a federally funded initiative called Iowa Safe and Supportive Schools. That program is providing at-risk schools with $14 million over three years to overhaul their social and academic climates. (Iowa was awarded the money along with 11 other states through a competitive grant process from the Office of Safe and Drug-free Schools).

In Louisiana, the model is the basis of an emerging program called the Comprehensive Learning Supports System. Districts that follow the model, like Sabine Parish, draw heavily on the enabling component concept via a statewide blueprint that spells out the ingredients of the model and how to implement it. State education leaders are currently presenting on the model and disseminating it throughout the state, as well as providing in-depth training when districts ask for it, says Louisiana Assistant State Superintendent Donna Nola-Ganey.

In Mobile, Ala., the framework received national recognition in the wake of Hurricane Katrina, thanks to a strong learning supports system already in place. Because the district's support services were so well organized, school personnel were able to respond quickly and effectively to the needs of disaster-affected children and their families, providing them with food, clothing and lodging and setting up provisional schools to help children keep on track with their studies, says Rhonda Neal-Waltman, EdD, then the city's assistant superintendent of student support services.

Examples of how the framework operates include managing cases family by family rather than child by child and requiring all school personnel to pitch in, regardless of position. "I didn't care what your title was—from A to Z, you were there to help that family," Neal-Waltman says.

The effort grabbed the attention of the children's educational publishing company Scholastic, which donated time, money and materials to spread the word about the enabling component nationwide. In partnership with Adelman and Taylor and the American Association of School Administrators, Scholastic's community affairs division is also helping to implement the model in four school districts in four states.

In addition, the National Association of School Psychologists is promoting the work nationally in several ways. For instance, the group summarized Adelman and Taylor's work in an advocacy document for educating local, state and national government officials. NASP leaders also met with U.S. Secretary of Education Arne Duncan to educate him on the model, and sponsored a congressional briefing on learning and social-emotional supports for military, foster and homeless children.

"For us, learning supports is really about trying to help folks understand that you don't think about kids' social and emotional needs as something you do after you address their academic achievement," says NASP Past President Kathleen M. Minke, PhD. "If you don't address their social and emotional needs as part of their whole school experience, you will never get the degree of academic achievement that our nation is seeking through school reform."

School districts that have embraced Adelman and Taylor's model are excited by its promise and its early results, though it's not an easy fix. If a district decides to "go all the way" and change its organizational charts to better integrate the enabling component into academics, for instance, it can mean new job titles, new job duties and other shake-ups, Neal-Waltman says.

"Did I have people who either had to get used to this change or get off the train?" she says. "Yes, I did."

Though this kind of widespread change is never easy, many hope the model can help stem the tide of high dropout rates, truancy and problem behaviors. Grant Parish, La., Superintendent Sheila Jackson, for example, says she hopes the restructuring can help address students' aggressive behaviors.

"We serve many children of poverty who have been raised to use physical aggression to resolve issues," she says. "And we're always being punitive rather than proactive."

She envisions the framework will teach educators more effective ways to help students communicate their needs and problems. "I'm not naïve enough to believe that we can change where they live or the culture they return to each day," she says, "but we can at least equip them with the skills to manage it better."

Meanwhile, Jackson, of Sabine Parish, says he's convinced the model will continue to improve children's psychosocial well-being and academic success.

"Eventually, we're going to be No. 1 in our state," he says. "And when we are, it will be because we're addressing the needs of the total child."

TEN

Foster Care Systems Can Only Help Teens Until They Age Out

Colleen Doescher-Train

Youth who are aging out of the foster care system face housing challenges. In the following viewpoint, Colleen Doescher-Train explains that policies and programs have been implemented in the past thirty years that help youth transitions into adulthood, such as Chafee Foster Care Independence Funds, and HUD vouchers. But the author argues that these have not been entirely successful; teens who have emancipated from foster care still lack the support they need to be successful. As a result, they are at greater risk for criminal activity, homelessness, unplanned pregnancies, not completing high school, or not attending college. Doescher-Train is a Child Protection Investigative Social Worker in Minneapolis, Minnesota.

The U.S. Department of Housing and Urban Development (HUD) released the report Housing for Youth Aging Out of Care in May 2014. This report details the housing challenges that youth who age out of the foster care system face. According to the report, several regional studies have shown that between 11 and 37 percent of these youth have experienced homelessness, while 25 to 50 percent have experienced housing instability (e.g. couch surfing, doubling up, eviction). A 2012 survey of homeless youth

"Housing supports for youth aging out of foster care," by Colleen Doescher-Train, Regents of the University of Minnesota, June 18, 2014. Reprinted by permission.

Teens who have aged out of foster care often lack the support they need to succeed on their own.

in Minnesota (conducted by Wilder Research) found that 35 percent had lived in a foster home, and 16 percent had left a social service placement within the past 12 months.

The authors outline four policies and programs that have been implemented in the past thirty years that are designed to help youth transition to adulthood:

1. Fostering Connections to Success and Increasing Adoptions Act of 2008: Extends the eligibility for Title IV-E funding for youth in the foster care system until the age of 21, as long as they meet certain criteria. To date, not all states have implemented this policy.

2. Chafee Foster Care Independence Program: Provides funding to youth for independent living services; however,

states may only use up to thirty percent of funds for costs related to housing.

3. Transitional Living Program: Funds are provided to youth ages 16-21 for longer term housing and supportive services.

4. Education and Training Voucher Program: Provides youth who qualify to receive Chafee funds with up to 5,000 dollars per year to attend a qualified postsecondary institution. This stipend can be used for housing.

The article also outlines HUD's key programs and policies that are designed to provide this population with housing support. These programs can be combined with other programs in most states.

1. Public housing and the Housing Choice Voucher (HCV): This program was previously known as Section 8. Through this program, tenants typically have their rent subsidized to thirty percent of their adjusted gross income. Each public housing authority may give preference to former foster youth. Unfortunately, the waiting list in many communities in the US is often very long or even closed. Typically, this program does not combine the voucher with housing supports that youth formerly in foster care often need.

2. Continuum of Care: HUD awards competitive annual grants to local agencies across the US that address homelessness through various coordinated processes in the community.

3. Family Unification Program (FUP): FUP is a relatively small HCV program. As of fall 2013, 242 PHAs administered approximately 20,500 FUP vouchers. The primary focus of the program is to subsidize housing for families who are at imminent risk of having their children placed in out-of-home care due to lack of adequate housing. FUP may also be utilized by youth who left foster care at age 16 or older who do not have adequate housing. The report notes that though FUP has shown good results for supporting these youth, the program is not widely used for youth.

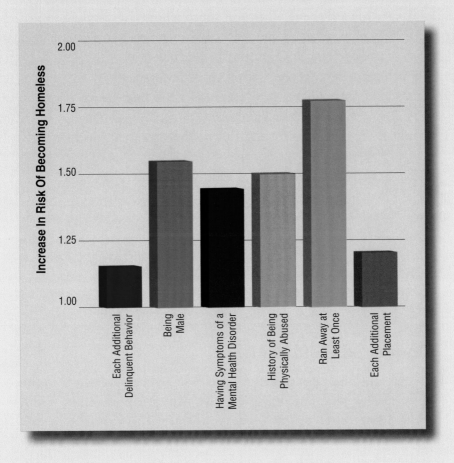

Predictors of homelessness among youths aging out of foster care

Increase In Risk Of Becoming Homeless

2.00

1.75

1.50

1.25

1.00

Each Additional Delinquent Behavior

Being Male

Having Symptoms of a Mental Health Disorder

History of Being Physically Abused

Ran Away at Least Once

Each Additional Placement

Source: Chapin Hall, University of Chicago

The report discusses the promise of the Family Unification Program in supporting former foster youth. Public child welfare agencies, or the partners with whom they contract, are required to offer supportive services to all youth who receive the FUP voucher. The purpose of providing these services to youth is to help youth develop the skills necessary to live independently. The supportive services include (but are not limited to) money management training, proper nutrition, employment counseling, and how to work with landlords to help youth obtain and keep their housing while receiving the voucher and afterwards.

The authors note that the program has limited vouchers to allocate toward the families and youth whom the program serves. Additionally, the FUP voucher for former foster youth limits the use of the voucher to 18 months and is only for youth ages 18-21. Vouchers previously used by youth do not necessarily get re-allocated to other youth as they can also go to families. Families, on the other hand, do not have time limits; thus the turnover for families receiving this voucher is much lower than it is for youth. Due to these constraints, currently only 14 percent of households who receive the voucher are former foster youth.

There are various other promising programs discussed within the report that are specific to communities and states across the U.S., including Restoration Gardens (Baltimore, MD), Youth Moving On (Pasadena, CA), and Transitional Housing Program for Emancipated Foster Youth (CA). These programs also couple housing assistance with supportive services for former foster youth.

Impact on Child Welfare

Numerous empirical research articles have been published in the past decade that detail the negative experiences faced by youth who have emancipated from foster care without the supports needed to transition successfully. The negative outcomes that are often associated with this transition include:

- Increased risk of involvement in the criminal justice system
- Increased risk of becoming homeless
- Increased risk to experience unplanned pregnancy
- Reduced likelihood of completing high school
- Reduced likelihood of attending and graduating from college

Research has also shown that there are benefits to having safe and stable housing:

> [I]n addition to meeting the basic human need for shelter, housing that is safe and stable can function as a platform that promotes positive outcomes across a range of domains from education to employment to physical and mental health.

By increasing access to housing support and supportive services for youth aging out of foster care, the authors of this report hope to help youth overcome some of these negative outcomes.

ELEVEN

Foster Caregivers Face Challenges with Teen Victims of Abuse and Exploitation

Child Welfare Information Gateway

Homeless teens who have experienced sexual abuse and exploitation can have an especially difficult time transitioning to a safe home. In the following viewpoint, the experts at Child Welfare Information Gateway illustrate the challenges faced by kinship caregivers, or foster, or adoptive parents of a young teen who has been sexually abused. Young teens who have been abused may demonstrate behaviors that are excessive or aggressive. But, the authors argue, things can be done to help ensure that any child visiting or living in the home experiences a structured, safe, and nurturing environment. A service of the US Department of Health and Human Services, Child Welfare Information Gateway promotes the safety and well being of children, youth, and families.

If you are parenting a child who has been removed from his or her family, you may not know for sure whether or not the child in your care has been sexually abused. Child welfare agencies usually share all known information about your child's history with you; however, there may be no prior record of abuse, and many children do not disclose past abuse until they feel safe. For this

Source: Child Welfare Information Gateway (2013). Parenting a child who has been sexually abused: A guide for foster and adoptive parents. Washington, DC: U.S. Department of Health and Human Services, Children's Bureau.

Emotional scars from previous experiences, like past sexual abuse, make it difficult for homeless teens to feel safe again.

reason, kinship caregivers or foster or adoptive parents are sometimes the first to learn that sexual abuse has occurred. Even when there is no documentation of prior abuse, you may suspect something happened because of your child's behavior.

Signs of Sexual Abuse

There are no hard and fast rules about what constitutes normal sexual development and what behaviors might signal sexual abuse. Children show a range of sexual behaviors and sexual curiosity at each developmental level, and their curiosity, interest,

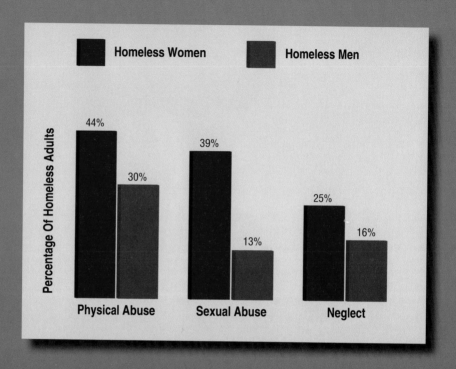

History of childhood abuse among homeless adults in Minnesota

■ Homeless Women   ■ Homeless Men

Percentage Of Homeless Adults

44%
30%
Physical Abuse

39%
13%
Sexual Abuse

25%
16%
Neglect

Source: Wilder Research

and experimentation may occur gradually, based on their development. However, children who have been sexually abused may demonstrate behaviors that are unusual, excessive, aggressive, or explicit. There is no one specific sign or behavior that can be considered proof that sexual abuse has definitively occurred, but there are a number of signs that are suggestive of abuse.

Factors Affecting the Impact of Sexual Abuse

If a professional has determined that a child in your care has been a victim of sexual abuse, or if you continue to suspect that the child in your care has been abused, it is important to understand how abusive experiences may affect children's behavior.

All children who have been sexually abused have had their physical and emotional boundaries violated or crossed in some way. Because of this, children may feel a lack of trust and safety with others. Children who have been abused may come to view the world as unsafe, and adults as manipulative and untrustworthy. As with other types of abuse or trauma, many factors influence how children think and feel about the abuse, how the abuse affects them, and how their recovery progresses.

It is very important for children to understand that they are not to blame for the abuse they experienced. Your family's immediate response to learning about the sexual abuse and ongoing acceptance of what the child has told you will play a critical role in your child's ability to recover and lead a healthy life.

Some parents may feel grave concern when children act out sexually with peers or younger children and may question why a child who has been abused, and suffered from that experience, could repeat it with someone else. Children who have experienced sexual abuse need an opportunity to process their own abuse in therapy or with a trusted trained adult to understand their thoughts and feelings and to have a chance to ask questions and achieve some kind of closure. Acting-out behaviors usually indicate that some traumatic impact of their abuse is still active and signals a need for additional attention. Responding in calm, informed ways while seeking appropriate professional help for children whose acting out persists will be important to resolving children's sexual behavior problems. The most important lesson is learning not to over- or under-respond to problem situations and finding just the right balance of guidance and empathic care.

If your child has a history of prior abuse, it's important to know that he or she may be vulnerable to acting out victim or victimizing behaviors. Some children may be more likely to be bullied or exploited, and others may be angry and aggressive towards others. You may need to pay special attention to protecting some children while setting firm limits on others. In addition, some children act out when memories of their own abuse are triggered. Triggers can happen unexpectedly, for example, by seeing someone who looks like the abuser or in a situation such as being alone in a public restroom, or by a variety of circumstances that occur in daily life. Other triggers might include the scent of a particular cologne or shampoo or the texture of a particular piece of clothing or blanket.

In addition, there are cultural differences among children with regard to their comfort level with physical proximity, physical affection, bathing and nudity practices, hygiene, and other factors that can lead to problem situations. There are many cultures in which parents never discuss sexuality directly with their children, or in which any type of sexual activity can be viewed as unacceptable or punishable. Children may thus carry shame and guilt about their bodies.

Establishing Family Guidelines for Safety and Privacy

There are things you can do to help ensure that any child visiting or living in your home experiences a structured, safe, and nurturing environment. Some children who have been sexually abused may have a heightened sensitivity to certain situations. Making your home a comfortable place for children who have been sexually abused can mean changing some habits or patterns of family life. Incorporating some of these guidelines may also help reduce foster or adoptive parents' vulnerability to abuse allegations by children living with them.

Consider whether the following tips may be helpful in your family's situation:

- **Make sure every family member's comfort level with touching, hugging, and kissing is respected.** Do not force touching on children who seem uncomfortable being touched. Encourage children to respect the comfort and privacy of others.

- **Be cautious with playful touch, such as play fighting and tickling.** These may be uncomfortable or scary reminders of sexual abuse to some children.

- **Help children learn the importance of privacy.** Remind children to knock before entering bathrooms and bedrooms, and encourage children to dress and bathe themselves if they are able. Teach children about privacy and respect by modeling this behavior and talking about it openly.

- **Keep adult sexuality private.** Teenage siblings may need reminders about what is permitted in your home when boyfriends and girlfriends are present. Adult caretakers will also need to pay special attention to intimacy and sexuality when young children with a history of sexual abuse are underfoot.

- **Be aware of and limit sexual messages received through the media.** Children who have experienced sexual abuse can find sexual content overstimulating or disturbing. It may be helpful to monitor music and music videos, as well as television programs, video games, and movies containing nudity, sexual activity, or sexual language. Limit access to grownup magazines and monitor children's Internet use. In addition, limit violent graphic or moving images in TV or video games.

- **Supervise and monitor children's play.** If you know that your child has a history of sexual abuse, it will be important to supervise and monitor his or her play with siblings or other children in your home. This means having children play within your view and not allowing long periods of time when children are unsupervised. Children may have learned about sexual abuse from others and may look for times to explore these activities with other children if left unsupervised. It will be important for parents and caretakers to be cautious but avoid feeling paranoid.

- **Prepare and develop comfort with language about sexual boundaries.** It will be important for you to be proactive in developing and practicing responses to children who exhibit sexual behavior problems. Many parents feel uncomfortable addressing the subject so they ignore or avoid direct discussions. Because there are so many differences in the messages parents want to convey to their children, it is useful to prepare ahead and be proactive. If your child has touching problems *(or any sexually aggressive behaviors)*, you may need to take additional steps to help ensure safety for your child as well as his or her peers. Consider how these tips may apply to your own situation:

- **With friends.** If your child has known issues with touching other children, you will need to ensure supervision when he or she is playing with friends, whether at your home or theirs. Sleepovers may not be a good idea when children have touching problems.

- **At school.** You may wish to inform your child's school of any inappropriate sexual behavior, to ensure an appropriate level of supervision. Often this information can be kept confidential by a school counselor or other personnel.

- **In the community.** Supervision becomes critical any time children with sexual behavior problems are with groups of children.

Impact of Sexual Abuse on the Family

Being a kinship caregiver or a foster or adoptive parent to a child who has experienced sexual abuse can be stressful to marriages and relationships. Parenting in these situations may require some couples to be more open with each other and their children about sexuality in general and sexual problems specifically. If one parent is more involved in addressing the issue than another, the imbalance can create difficulties in the parental relationship. A couple's sexual relationship can also be affected, if sex begins to feel like a troubled area of the family's life. If and when these problems emerge, it is often helpful to get professional advice.

In addition, if one parent was more in favor of adopting, and the other parent merely complied, general stress can be added to the couple when children have a range of problem behaviors that require attention. Some parents develop resentful and angry or withdrawn feelings toward foster or adoptive children who take up a lot of time and energy *(for example, children who need extra monitoring and supervision or transport to weekly therapy appointments).*

Parents can also feel stress because the child's siblings *(birth, foster, or adoptive)* may be exposed to new or focused attention on sexuality that can be challenging for them. If one child is acting out sexually, you may need to talk with siblings about what they see, think, and feel, as well as how to respond. Children may also need to be coached on what *(and how much)* to say about their sibling's problems to their friends. If your children see that you are actively managing the problem, they will feel more secure and will worry less.

When one child has been sexually abused, parents often become very protective of their other children. It is important to find a balance between reasonable worry and overprotectiveness. Useful strategies to prevent further abuse may include teaching children to stand up for themselves, talking with them about being in charge of their bodies, and fostering open communication with your children.

TWELVE

Communities Should Build More Homeless Shelters

Rachel Lippmann

> Many cities across the US and around the world struggle to solve the problem of homelessness. In the following viewpoint Rachel Lippman uses the city of St. Louis, Missouri, as an example of the issues urban leaders face. St. Louis County devised a 10-year plan to battle homelessness. However, implementing the plan has proven more challenging than expected. The details of how governments work with agencies and ministries, often getting caught up in bureaucracy, to address the issue of homelessness may shed light on why the problem is so difficult to solve. Lippmann is a journalist for St. Louis Public Radio.

This winter, St. Louis County did something it hadn't done before—it opened a temporary shelter where homeless men and women could go to get out of the cold. It's a small piece of a 10-year plan to battle homelessness that St. Louis City and County signed onto in 2004. But obstacles remain to implementing the rest of the ideas in that document.

What is "homelessness?"

Per the 2009 HEARTH (Homeless Emergency Assistance and Rapid Transition to Housing) Act, a person is considered homeless

"Access, Attitude Make It Tough To Address Homelessness In St. Louis County," Rachel Lippmann, St. Louis Public Radio, February 12, 2014. Reprinted by permission.

Homeless shelters are only a small part of the solution to a much larger problem.

if they lack a "fixed, regular and adequate" nighttime residence. This includes sleeping in a place not ordinarily meant as overnight accommodations (like a public park, train or bus station, or a car). Individuals living in temporary shelters are also homeless, as are those at risk of losing their homes.

Anyone fleeing a life-threatening situation or domestic violence is considered homeless if they do not have the resources to obtain other housing.

How does the county find those who might be homeless?

Some people self-identify when they call the housing crisis hotline for Housing Resource Center, part of the Catholic Charities of St. Louis. In 2013, 647 people who called the hotline were homeless individuals needing help to find a place to stay and other services. The hotline also provides resources to help people avoid losing their homes.

Additionally, the county is required by federal law to participate in a "point-in-time" count, which is a one-day census of the homeless population. The 2014 PIT for St. Louis County took place on Jan. 30.

How accurate are the PIT numbers?

It depends which category you look at. For people in emergency shelter and transitional housing programs, the numbers are fairly accurate because they come directly from the agencies providing the services who know how many clients they have on that given day. The count of unsheltered individuals, however, is often done by driving to "hot spots" in a given area and identifying those who might be homeless.

There are several pitfalls to the method of counting the unsheltered people. In the county especially, it can be hard to locate those who are homeless. Many are not out on the street, but are instead staying with friends and family, staying in a hotel, or living in their cars.

Out on the street, identifying a potentially homeless individual calls for a lot of guesswork based somewhat on stereotypes. For example, a volunteer with the county census last year approached a young woman pushing a shopping cart full of laundry. She turned out not to be homeless, but understood why someone would ask about her housing status.

The time of day can impact the results as well. The county's 2014 count began at 10 a.m., which is not the best time to do so, according to Shana Eubanks, the county's homeless services manager. As she it explained it, the homeless want to be up and moving before the commuters. By late morning, they're already working to make themselves invisible.

The time of year is also a factor. Anyone is more likely to be lingering outside when the temperature isn't in the single digits - which is why the state of Missouri helps arrange summer counts. The winter count is federally mandated.

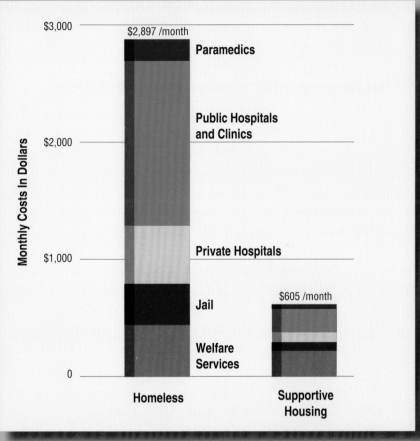

Average costs per month for a homeless person in Los Angeles versus a person in supportive "Housing First" housing

Monthly Costs In Dollars

$3,000

$2,897 /month

Paramedics

Public Hospitals and Clinics

$2,000

$1,000

Private Hospitals

$605 /month

Jail

Welfare Services

0

Homeless

Supportive Housing

Source: Economic Roundtable, via Mother Jones

What services are available for the homeless once they are counted?

Someone who calls the housing crisis hotline is first directed toward an emergency shelter, the location of which is based on the caller's last known address. In addition to a bed and meals, the emergency shelters provide medical screenings, assistance with job applications, and other social support.

In 2013, the county helped fund 185 emergency shelter beds, plus another 255 transitional housing beds. A majority of the beds are located within the county boundaries. However, single men must travel into the city to Peter and Paul Community Services to find a place to stay on an emergency basis. And many of the other support services for the homeless, such as childcare or medical services, are also only located in the city. That can necessitate two-hour trips on a bus.

What happens once someone is off the street?

Since 2009, federal law has prioritized a "housing-first model"— that is, getting individuals a place to stay first, then providing the social services support necessary. In government-speak, it's called permanent supportive housing, and the county provides the funds for about 400 of those beds.

That's not nearly enough. And this is where NIMBY (Not In My Back Yard) becomes a problem again. Landlords, said Shana Eubanks, the county's homeless services manager, are worried about setting aside units for people who might be less-than-ideal tenants because of addiction and other mental health issues. And building new permanent supportive housing units requires either the support of a municipality, or the county funding an appropriate location in unincorporated areas.

THIRTEEN

Homeless Shelters Encourage People to Be Lazy, Increase Crime, and Lower Home Values

Erika Aguilar

> Proposals to build homeless shelters are often protested by
> area residents worried about the effects such shelters will
> have on their neighborhoods, including raising crime rates
> and lowering property values. In the following viewpoint,
> Erika Aguilar examines the negative reaction of residents
> of Anaheim, California, to plans to build a nearby shelter.
> Despite a growing homeless population, most residents adopt
> the NIMBY (not in my backyard) stance. While county offi-
> cials have experienced tremendous difficulty finding commu-
> nities willing to host any type of homeless services, proponents
> argue the shelter will improve the surrounding area. Aguiar is
> an independent radio reporter and producer.

Orange County supervisors are holding a public hearing
November 17 about plans to build a shelter with up to 200
beds located at 1000 N. Kraemer Place in a light industrial area of
Anaheim. Among the points of discussion will be ways the shelter
operators can placate neighbors who've been holding community
meetings to organize against the shelter and plopping signs in their
yards protesting the choice of site.

"Homeless shelters struggle to fit into neighborhoods," by Erika Aguilar, Southern California Public Radio, November 5, 2015. Reprinted by Pprmission.

Some communities fight the existence of homeless shelters, believing such services increase crime and lower property values.

KPCC's studios, has found a way to coexist with retail, businesses, residents, and a daycare next door. Volunteers and staff at the shelter pick up trash on surrounding streets. When a rowdy group this year attracted to the shelter's meals drew complaints, officials changed the organization's policy to only serve people who enroll in programs.

In Long Beach, the 200-bed Long Beach Rescue Mission hasn't always had the best relationship with the city, said Executive Director Chaplain Robert Probst, but it's made strides by providing services to the neighborhood.

"The way we present it is so important because it shouldn't be a deterrent," he said. "It should be a light. It should be a breath of hope."

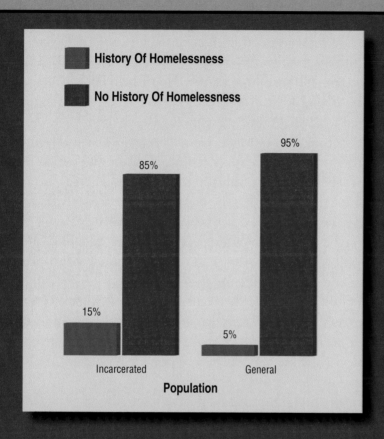

History of homelessness among inmates versus general population

- History Of Homelessness
- No History Of Homelessness

95%

85%

15%

5%

Incarcerated   General

Population

Source: National HCH Council

The shelter's meal schedule works around the class schedule of the middle school across the street. Shelter staff and clients staying there keep the homeless from camping in the adjacent park. And residents of the parking-strapped neighborhood are allowed to use the Mission's lot after hours.

Parents and young skateboarders living near the Mission have mixed feelings about the shelter. Some would rather not have homeless people in the neighborhood – they ask for free cigarettes or stare at kids – but residents say they feel crime has gone down compared to five or ten years ago.

"My kids haven't had an issue coming to the skate park or the park," said Marlene Robles who has lived in neighborhood for five years. "It's just with certain homeless (persons) that come up to them and try to say hi."

A commanding officer for the Long Beach Police Department said the department does not track homeless-related crime and declined to discuss crime surrounding the shelter.

In Pasadena, Lt. Mark Goodman of the Pasadena Police Department said he's hesitant to link crime around Union Station to the homeless shelter. But the general public seems to be making that link. About a third of the department's calls each day involve the homeless--but they don't necessarily involve crimes.

"Maybe they began as a report of a suspected crime," he said. "Our officers get there, they find there's no crime that took place, or it's a completely different type of incident."

In Orange County, the Anaheim Police Department is promising extra patrols and surveillance cameras in the area surrounding the proposed 200-bed homeless shelter in The Canyon area. On-site private security will also be provided, Orange County officials said at the September meeting.

Proponents argue the shelter will actually improve the surrounding area. Officials say the shelter operator will be required to hold quarterly advisory board meetings that residents and business owners can sit on and the public can attend.

There's no data to support the idea that shelters ruin neighborhoods, homeless advocate Larry Hanes told the crowd gathered at a recent community meeting.

"But what the data does support is that shelter linked to housing ends homelessness," he said.

That argument, however, hasn't swayed many, like Michael Chew, a real estate agent who lives across the freeway, less than a mile from the proposed shelter site. Chew is with the Orange-Riverdale Homeowners Alliance that opposes the shelter site.

He said homeless camps have grown along the nearby Santa Ana River Trail and worries when the homeless shelter gets full, people will choose to sleep along the trail or in his neighborhood. And then, there's no turning back.

"If it doesn't work out or if the shelter becomes problematic, is the county going to close the shelter then," Chew questioned. "Or will it always be a problem for us going forward."

FOURTEEN

The Homeless May Not Be Ready for a Home

Babysteps Ministry

> Conventional wisdom points to providing free or affordable housing as the solution to the homelessness problem. However, as Babysteps Ministry suggests in the following viewpoint, providing help to individuals to reestablish their lives first is more effective than spending capital resources to bestow housing upon the homeless. The authors argue that somebody who's been trained by the system to have things done for them cannot be expected to suddenly handle having their own place. Thus, it is important to prepare the homeless for the big change of having a home, and all that entails, before they can adapt to the responsibility. Babysteps Ministry is a Seattle-based nonprofit working to eradicate homelessness.

It's a common argument – if we just get homeless people into housing, then we're solving homelessness. And on a surface level, it makes sense. Homeless means "without a home." So give them a home, and they're no longer homeless.

If only it were that simple.

Councilman Tim Burgess wrote a guest column in the *Seattle Times* in August, 2016, and he argued for a reworking of how we fund the various services that try to help homeless people in Seattle and King County.

He made a number of good points – especially this question:

"Seattle City Councilman says 'Housing First' is Key to Solving Homelessness. But Is That the Answer?" Babysteps Ministry, Reprinted by permission.

After years of living on the streets, formerly homeless people need support to help them transition to having a home.

"Are we investing our resources wisely to achieve the best possible results?"

We agree with his answer to his own question. Not just Seattle, but most of the country is failing to use their resources wisely to truly help people trapped in homelessness.

The problem is – some of Burgess' own solutions still miss the mark. He says "housing first" should be our top priority, as quickly as possible. Again, this sounds reasonable. But this is actually just another way to spend a ton of money and not see significant change.

At Babysteps Ministry, here's the question we ask every day with regard to the homeless people we talk with:

What does it really take to get someone off the streets – permanently?

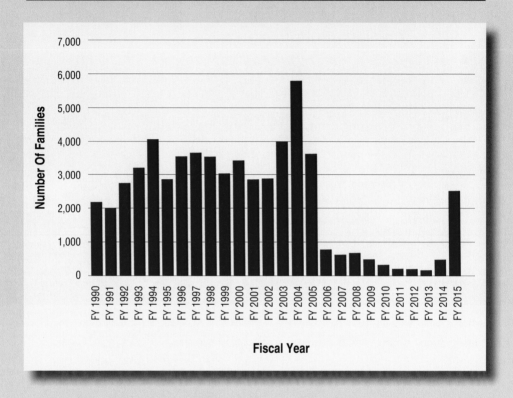

Number of New York City homeless families placed into permanent federal housing (Public Housing and Section 8), fiscal years 1990–2015

Source: Coalition for the Homeless

Consider just this partial list of services and giveaways currently available to homeless people:

- Free emergency shelters
- Affordable housing
- Rent assistance
- Free counseling, for addiction and other struggles
- Drug rehab
- Free legal assistance

- Free bus tickets
- Free cell phone service
- Free meals
- Free water
- Free blankets
- Free clothes, shoes, socks, jackets, underwear, pants, and more – often for the same people over and over again

These things are given away on a daily basis to the more than 10,000 homeless people currently living on the streets of Seattle. And yet, there are more homeless people each year. That should bother you.

Ask yourself:

If I were given all those things for free, what would my life be like?

You might start thinking of how much money you could save, or the new house or car you could buy, or something you've been wanting to do but couldn't afford. That list covers the majority of our lifetime expenses, including the big ones! Except perhaps for college education.

So, we must admit that something is off here, and ask one final question: If homeless people are being given such an astonishing amount of free goods and services – why do they stay homeless?

Why Do They Stay Homeless?

Here's where we get a little offensive. They stay homeless because they're not ready for a home.

A superb movie that dramatizes this perfectly is called *The Soloist*, starring Jamie Fox and Robert Downey Jr. If you've never seen this film, and believe "housing first" is the answer, we challenge you to go watch it. It's a true story.

Downey plays a reporter who encounters a homeless man (Fox), who is also a musical virtuoso. Downey can't stand the fact this supremely talented man is on the streets, so he starts doing whatever he can to help the guy, including renting him an apartment for free. How Fox's character handles this free home – and

Downey's friendship, at first – offers a rare glimpse into the real challenges to truly helping many of the people who are homeless.

For many of them, just giving them homes ultimately solves nothing. If this weren't true, then why do the "one night count" numbers keep increasing, in spite of all the services and money we're spending? Clearly – what we're doing now is not working. And the reason it's not working isn't because we aren't prioritizing "housing first."

The reason is because the causes of persistent homelessness are far more complicated than a key and a one-bedroom apartment will be able to fix.

Yes – some people are ready to handle a home. And Burgess is correct about this part. Some people end up in homelessness, but are determined not to stay there, and will take advantage of whatever services they can find to get back on their feet. For people like that, many of Burgess' solutions will work.

But it's the chronically homeless. The truly destitute. The ones who have lost hope, who are used to being overlooked and ignored. The ones with criminal records and no job skills. These are the people who simply aren't ready for a home. You give them one, and they will trash it.

But they don't trash it out of malice or disrespect in every instance. In most cases, it's simply too much responsibility.

Picture this:

Suppose there's a person who's lived for ten years on the street. Ten years. A long time. He gotten free meals, free clothes, and access to free emergency shelters the whole time. Aid and nonprofit workers he visits now and then do everything for him. They make appointments for him. Fill out paperwork he needs. They do everything – even including dialing his phone and handing it back to him to call a particular service.

And now – suddenly – he's given a whole apartment all to himself.

He has to clean and use his own bathroom.

He has to keep up on his monthly expenses.

He has to buy his own food.

He has to cook his own food.

He has to answer his mail.

He has to make his own appointments.

We can go on forever. The point is – living your own life, even without a job, entails a ton of little minor tasks and responsibilities that YOU don't even think about. You just do them. Just ask a retired person.

But for someone who's been trained by the system to have things done for him, for years, he simply cannot be expected to suddenly handle the basic responsibilities that come with having his own place.

And that's why 'housing first' won't solve homelessness for many people on the streets. They need someone to walk with them. To come alongside them and re-empower them, one step at a time. They need help re-entering life.

They need someone, like Downey's character ultimately discovers, to be a true friend.

Homelessness can ultimately be boiled down to loneliness and extended isolation, combined with the great variety of hard circumstances that people face. With no one walking alongside them, they detach from human interactions and institutions, and end up on the street alone.

Babysteps Ministry believes in providing this kind of friendship. It's slower than a huge room full of free meals and blankets. It's less flashy than huge new affordable housing complexes. It won't get funded by any massive property tax levies.

But it works – and for the chronically homeless especially – it's the only thing that really works. It's helping homeless people take one step at a time, when they really want to take it, to dig a little bit higher out of the hole they've fallen into.

Do you want to solve homelessness? It's not housing first. It's people first.

What You Should Know About Teen Homelessness

Facts About Teen Homelessness

- Each year more than two million youth in America will face a period of homelessness.

- Almost 40% of the U.S. homeless population is under 18 years old.

- According to HUD's 2014 point-in-time report, 34% of the total homeless population is under 24 years old.

- Some homeless children and youth are with their families. In 2014, 45,205 were unaccompanied.

- The Department of Justice estimates that each year more than 1.7 million teens experience homelessness in the United States.

- Unaccompanied homeless youth represent 7% of the total homeless population in the U.S. (HUD, 2015).

- On a single night in 2015, there were approximately 36,907 unaccompanied homeless youth throughout all of the U.S. (HUD, 2015).

- 87% or 32,240 individuals were youth between the ages of 18 and 24 years old (HUD, 2015)

- 13% or 3,667 individuals were children under 18 years old (HUD, 2015).

- Youth 12 to 17 years old are more at risk of homelessness than adults.

- Between 1.7 and 2.8 million runaway and homeless youth live on the street each year.

- Staff at runaway and homeless shelters report that 63% of the runaways that they work with are depressed, 50% have problems at school, 20% have drug and alcohol abuse problems, and 17% have been in the juvenile justice system.
- 57% of homeless kids spend at least one day every month without food.

Factors for Teen Homelessness

- The historical and current impact of racism has limited the access to affordable housing and living wage employment for people of color.
- More than 25% of former foster children became homeless within two to four years of leaving the system.
- 46% of runaway and homeless youth reported being physically abused, 38% reported being emotionally abused, and 17% reported being forced into unwanted sexual activity by a family or household member.
- According to a study of youth in shelters, nearly 50% reported intense conflict or physical harm by a family member as a major contributing factor to their being homeless.
- A 2002 report prepared for the U.S. Department of Health and Human Services, on sexual abuse among teen runaways found that 21 to 40% of homeless youth had been sexually abused compared to 1 to 3% of the general youth population.
- A report by the Office of Juvenile Justice and Delinquency Prevention found 21% of runaway/throwaway kids had physical or sexual abuse in their history, or were afraid of suffering abuse if they went home.
- About 80% of homeless youth (12-21 years) use drugs and alcohol as a means of self-medication to deal with the traumatic experiences and abuse they face.

- Between 20 and 40% of homeless youth identify as LGBTQ
- Family rejection on the basis of sexual orientation and gender identity was the most frequently cited factor contributing to LGBTQ homelessness (46%).
- 75% of runaways are female.
- Estimates of the number of pregnant homeless girls are between 6 and 22%.
- Nearly half of youth on the street and a third of youth in shelters report having been pregnant in the past.

Facts About Teen Homelessness and Society

In the U.S. as many as 20,000 kids are forced into prostitution by human-trafficking networks each year.

- 26% of those in shelters and 32% of those on the street had attempted suicide.
- 75% of homeless and runaway youth have dropped out of school.
- 37% of homeless youth and 23% of runaway youth do not attend school.

Homeless children face many barriers to education, including:

- The inability to meet enrollment requirements (including requirements to provide proof of residency and legal guardianship, and school and health records);
- High mobility resulting in lack of school stability and educational continuity;
- Lack of transportation;
- Lack of school supplies and clothing;
- Lack of awareness and support from school staff; and
- Poor health, fatigue, and hunger.
- 50% of adolescents out of foster care and juvenile justice systems will be homeless within six months because they

are unprepared to live independently and have limited education and no social support.

- Youth experience unstable foster care placements or are discharged from foster care due to age.

- Over 50% of young people in shelters and on the streets report their parents told them to leave or knew they were leaving and did not care.

- Due to a lack of affordable, safe, and stable housing, youth may spend time in unstable temporary housing options, including family shelters, before becoming unaccompanied.

- According to the Urban Institution, nearly 20% of youths under 18 years old will run away at least once.

- One in seven people between 10 and 18 years old will run away.

- Of youth who run away, 41% have been abandoned by their parents for at least 24 hours and 43% have been beaten by a caretaker.

What You Should Do
About Teen Homelessness

What can you do to help put an end to teen homelessness? There are several ways to get involved in your community to support the cause.

First, educate yourself about the topic. Research its causes and become more aware of its symptoms. Find out the extent of the teen homelessness problem in your own city. Start to communicate with friends and classmates on the subject of teen homelessness. Discuss the issues with them to see if you can come up with ways to help out together.

Locate and contact some homeless shelters in your area to find out if there are any opportunities to volunteer at one, even if in just a small way. Does your church, or any other local faith based organization, have an outreach ministry to serve the needs of the homeless teen?

Homeless shelters are always seeking donations of blankets, clothing, personal hygiene items, and even school supplies. Start a campaign to begin collecting these types of things to donate. Begin fundraising to purchase additional items such as bus passes and gift cards for fast food and grocery stores. Ways to raise money include lemonade sales; bake and candy sales, car washes, and mowing lawns. Partner with local youth groups to help in these efforts.

Explore the possibilities of online activism. Look for websites that combine the efforts of youth across America. Join social media campaigns to help end the problem by contacting politicians who are in a position to enact legislation.

If you know of someone who is thinking of dropping out of school or running away, strongly encourage them to change their mind. The best way to end teen homelessness is to prevent it from happening in the first place. And just knowing that someone else cares about them, and what happens to them, might be all it takes to save someone from that fate.

ORGANIZATIONS TO CONTACT

The editors have compiled the following list of organizations concerned with the issues debated in this book. The descriptions are derived from materials provided by the organizations. All have publications or information available for interested readers. The list was compiled on the date of publication of the present volume; the information provided here may change. Be aware that many organizations take several weeks or longer to respond to inquiries, so allow as much time as possible.

Child Trends
7315 Wisconsin Avenue, Suite 1200W
Bethesda, MD 20814
(240) 223-9200
website: www.childtrends.org
Child Trends is the nation's leading nonprofit research organization focused exclusively on improving the lives and prospects of children, youth, and their families.

Covenant House
461 Eight Avenue
New York, NY 10001
(800) 388-3888
website: www.covenanthouse.org
Covenant House strives to be knowledge leaders in the field of homeless youth services. They share statistics on homeless youth in the U.S. in hope to inform other service providers, impact policy decisions, and engage people who want to help end youth homelessness.

National Alliance to End Homelessness
1518 K Street, 2nd floor
Washington, DC 20005
(202) 638-1526
website: www.endhomelessness.org

The National Alliance to End Homelessness works toward ending homelessness by improving homelessness policy, building on-the-ground capacity, and educating opinion leaders.

National Children's Advocacy Center (NCAC)
210 Pratt Avenue NE
Huntsville, AL 35801
(256) 533-KIDS (5437)
website: www.nationalcac.org
The NCAC serves as a model for the 950+ children's advocacy centers operating in the U.S. and in more than 25 countries throughout the world. The NCAC models, promotes, and delivers excellence in child abuse response and prevention through service, education, and leadership.

National Coalition for the Homeless (NCH)
2201 P Street NW
Washington, DC 20037-1033
(202) 462-4822
website: www.nationalhomeless.org
The NCH is a national network committed to a single mission: To prevent and end homelessness while ensuring the immediate needs of those experiencing homelessness are met and their civil rights protected.

National Human Trafficking Hotline (NHTH)
(888) 373-7888 or text @ befree (233733)
website: www.humantraffickinghotline.org
NHTH is a national anti-trafficking hotline serving victims and survivors of human trafficking and the anti-trafficking community in the U.S. The toll-free hotline is available to answer calls from anywhere in the country 24 hours a day, 7 days a week, every day of the year in more than 200 languages.

National Institute of Mental Health (NIMH)
6001 Executive Boulevard, Room 6200, MSC 9663
Bethesda, MD 20892-9663
(866) 6156464

website: www.nimh.nih.gov
NIMH funds and conducts research to help answer important scientific question about mental health. NIMH also communicates with scientists, patients, providers, and the general public about the science of mental health based on the latest research.

National Runaway Safeline (NRS)

3141B N. Lincoln
Chicago, IL 60657
(800) 786-2929
website: www.1800runaway.org
In an effort to help youth develop coping skills to avoid unsafe situations, the NRS provides educational tools and promotional materials for schools and youth-serving agencies. Their services are confidential and non-judgmental.

Substance Abuse and Mental Health Services Administration (SAMHSA)

5600 Fishers Lane
Rockville, MD 20857
(877) SAMHSA-7 (877-726-4727)
website: www.samhsa.gov
SAMHSA leads the public health efforts to advance the behavioral health of the nation. SAMHSA's mission is to reduce the impact of substance abuse and mental illness on America's communities.

United States Interagency Council on Homelessness

1275 First Street NE, Ste 227
Washington, DC
(202) 708-4663
website: www.usich.gov
The U.S. Interagency Council on Homelessness leads the national effort to prevent and end homelessness in America. They drive action among their 19 federal member agencies and foster partnerships at every level of government and with the private sector.

BIBLIOGRAPHY

Books

Jennifer Bringle, *Homelessness in America Today*. New York, NY: Rosen Publishing Group, 2010.

A.M. Buckley, *Homelessness*. Edina, MN: ABDO Publishing Company, 2012.

Kathy Furgang, *Ending Hunger and Homelessness Through Service Learning*. New York, NY: Rosen Publishing Group, 2015.

Arthur Gillard, *Issues That Concern You: Homelessness*. Detroit, MI: Greenhaven Press, 2012.

Ted Gottfried, *Homelessness: Whose Problem Is It?* Brookfield, CT: Millbrook Press 1999.

Pat LaMarche, *Left Out in America: The State of Homelessness in the United States*. Carlisle, PA: Charles Bruce Foundation, 2012.

Marcia Amidon Lusted, *I Am Homeless, Now What?* New York, NY: Rosen Publishing Group, 2017.

Noel Merino, *Poverty and Homelessness*. Farmington Hills, MI: Greenhaven Press, 2014.

Kevin Ryan and Tina Kelly, *Almost Home: Helping Kids Move from Homelessness to Hope*. Hoboken, NJ: John Wiley and Sons, Inc., 2012.

Tamara Thompson, *Opposing Viewpoints: Homelessness*. Detroit, MI: Greenhaven Press, 2012.

Jennifer Toth, *The Mole People: Life in the Tunnels Beneath New York City*. Chicago, IL: Chicago Review Press, 1993.

Jason Adams Wasserman and Jeffery Michael Clair, *At Home on the Street: People, Poverty, and a Hidden Culture of Homelessness*. Boulder, CO / London: Lynne Rienner, 2010.

Periodicals and Internet Sources

John Bridgeland & Bruce Reed, "*Homeless Kids is a Problem We Can Solve*," USA Today, June 15, 2016. https://www.usatoday.com/story/opinion/2016/06/15/youth-homelessness-education-schools-column/85834556.

Emma Brown, "*These are the Faces of America's Growing Youth Homeless Population,*" The Washington Post, June 17, 2016. https://www.washingtonpost.com/news/education/wp/2016/06/17/these-are-the-faces-of-americas-growing-youth-homeless-population/?utm_term=.0eeb11ef3d59.

Devon Haynie, "*Human Trafficking's High Toll on Homeless Youth,*" U.S. News, April 17, 2017. https://www.usnews.com/news/best-countries/articles/2017-04-17/homeless-youth-in-the-us-and-canada-face-high-rates-of-human-trafficking.

Judy Lightfoot, "*5 Ways to End Youth Homelessness,*" Crosscut.com, February 27, 2013. http://crosscut.com/2013/02/ending-youth-homelessness-5-top-ideas-naeh.

Raychelle Cassada Lohmann, "*Homeless Teens,*" Psychology Today, January 9, 2011. https://www.psychologytoday.com/blog/teen-angst/201101/homeless-teens.

Craig Phillips, "*Homeless but Not Hopeless: Homeless Youth in America,*" Independent Lens, April 9, 2015. http://www.pbs.org/independentlens/blog/homeless-but-not-hopeless-homeless-youth-in-america.

Terrance F. Ross, "*Young, Homeless – and Invisible,*" The Atlantic, February 11, 2015. https://www.theatlantic.com/education/archive/2015/02/young-homelessand-invisible/385355.

Andrew M, Seaman, "*Study Reveals No. 1 Cause of Youth Homelessness,*" Huffington Post, April, 6, 2016. http://www.huffingtonpost.com/entry/study-reveals-no-1-cause-of-youth-homelessness_us_57057deee4b053766188a3a5.

Jim Spellman, "*The Face of America's Homeless Youth,*" CNN, July 8, 2010. http://www.cnn.com/2010/LIVING/07/08/denver.homeless.youth/index.html.

Samantha Wender, "*A Teen Girl's Life on the Street,*" ABC News, January 28, 2011. http://abcnews.go.com/US/teen-girls-life-street/story?id=12780590.

Websites

Do Something
(www.dosomething.org)
A global movement for good, choose a campaign and take action with 5.5 million youth making positive change, both online and off. They're activating young people in every US area code and in 131 countries. You will team up with the people who have clothed half of America's youth in homeless shelters, for example.

KidsPeace
(www.kidspeace.org)
Founded in 1882, KidsPeace provides a unique psychiatric hospital; a comprehensive range of residential treatment programs; accredited educational services; and a variety of foster care and community-based treatment programs to help people in need overcome challenges and transform their lives. They provide emotional and physical health care and educational services in an atmosphere of teamwork, compassion, and creativity.

Safe Horizon
(www.safehorizon.org)
Established in 1978, it is the largest non-profit victim services agency in the US. It touches the lives of more than 250,000 individuals and families affected by crime and abuse throughout New York City each year. Safe Horizons partners with governmental and other community agencies and advocates for policies on a local, state, and national level on behalf of those affected by violence and abuse.

Youth
(www.youth.gov)
Youth.gov (formerly FindingYouthInfo.gov) was created by the Interagency Working Groups on Youth Programs (IWGYP), which is composed of representatives from 20 federal agencies that support programs and services focusing on youth and their needs.

Prayas Juvenile Aid Centre (JAC) Society, 45
pregnancy, 6, 68, 72
Probst, Robert, 88
prostitution, 6, 39, 44
PTSD, 11, 12, 13, 49
public housing, 38, 70

R
refugee children, 44
rehab, 94
rental assistance, 16, 38, 94
Resolution on the Plight of Street Children, 45
Restoration Gardens, 72
Robles, Marlene, 90
Runaway and Homeless Youth Act (RHYA), 5, 38
Ryan, Caitlin, 27

S
Scholastic, 66
Section 8, 70
sexism, 25
sexual abuse, 6, 74–81
sexual orientation, 6
shelters, 5, 7, 10, 15–17, 38, 40, 47, 48, 53, 55, 56, 57, 59, 82–86, 87–91
Skid Row, 9
social workers, 59, 68
soliciting, 6
Soloist, The, 95–96, 97
soup kitchens, 15
STDs, 6
stealing, 39, 44
stereotypes, 84
Street Kids International, 45
suicide, 5, 37, 51
Supportive Services for Veteran Families, 10

T
Taylor, Linda, 61, 63, 66
therapy, 12, 51, 77, 81
Title IV-E funding, 69
transitional housing, 5, 15, 70, 72, 84, 86
Transitional Housing Program for Emancipated Foster Youth, 72
Transitional Living Program, 70
transphobia, 25
truancy, 6, 67

U
unemployment, 17, 24, 29
UNICEF, 41
United Nations, 45
Urban Institute, 17
USAID, 40
US Conference of Mayors, 6
US Congress, 21, 23, 27, 33, 35, 46, 66
US Department of Education, 5
US Department of Health and Human Services, 19, 27, 74
US Department of Homeland Security, 6
US Department of Housing and Urban Development (HUD), 68, 70
US Department of Justice, 6
US Interagency Council on Homelessness, 51–52

V
veterans, 8–13, 49
Veterans Affairs (VA), 10, 12, 13
vouchers, 12, 68, 70–72

W
Washington Low Income Housing Alliance, 49
welfare checks, 16
welfare hotels, 5

Y
Youth Moving On, 72
youth of color (YOC), 25–32, 59
Youth Project, the, 51
Youth Risk Behavior Survey (YRBS), 27–28

PICTURE CREDITS